P9-DCZ-694

# RULERS IN
# PETTICOATS

# RULERS IN PETTICOATS

by
Mildred Boyd

Criterion Books
NEW YORK

BY THE SAME AUTHOR:
History in Harness: The Story of Horses
Black Flags and Pieces of Eight
The Silent Cities: Civilizations Lost and Found

# ACKNOWLEDGMENTS

The photographs in this book are reproduced through the courtesy of:

The British Information Bureau: Queen Elizabeth II, P. 206

All others from the picture collection of The New York Public Library

*In Memory of my father,*
JAMES E. WORTHY, SR.

# Contents

# Illustrations

# RULERS IN
# PETTICOATS

HATSHEPSUT ASCENDED THE EGYPTIAN
THRONE   1520 B.C.

# I

# HATSHEPSUT:
## "Lord" of the Two Lands

Civilization came early to the land of the Nile. While others wandered endlessly through forest and desert seeking the game or the grass which would keep them alive, the men of Egypt built their villages. To protect their precious strip of fertile land, tribe united with tribe, district with district. By 2700 B.C. the long, narrow valley was united under a single ruler who was a god as well as a king.

It is only fitting that such an ancient kingdom should produce the "first important woman in history."

Hatshepsut was a royal princess of the Eighteenth Dynasty—a very royal princess indeed. Her father was the great warrior-king, Thutmose I. Her mother was Ahmose, a descendant of the Theban princess who had driven the hated Hyksos kings from the land and restored Egyptian rule to Egypt.

Only through his wife could Thutmose lay claim to the throne. But with her he made himself absolute monarch of an empire. It was an empire which stretched from the Fourth Cataract of the Nile to the far reaches of the Euphrates.

But Thutmose had no sons by his royal wife. Only the Princess Hatshepsut, of all his children, was a true descendant of the house of Thebes. And there were many who considered these children the only legitimate claimants to the throne. It was for this reason that Thutmose was forced by his nobles to declare Hatshepsut his heir.

Even so, she would not be allowed to reign alone. She was married at a tender age to her half-brother, Thutmose II. The title to the throne might be hers, but the power and the glory would belong to her husband.

Perhaps Hatshepsut always resented this. She could hardly have helped knowing that she was not only royal, she was divine. To her it would have seemed only normal that her every wish was granted almost before she could express it. The glittering court in which she grew up was one of the wealthiest and most luxurious the world has ever known.

The little princess could summon hordes of slaves to do her bidding. Her apartments overflowed with exotic treasures. Her gardens were lush bowers of flowering shrubs and artificial waterways. Her garments were of the finest weave and her jewels were magnificant works of art. Her tables groaned with the rarest of delicate foods. And wherever she walked, the proudest men in the land prostrated themselves before her.

Small wonder then that Hatshepsut grew into a willful and headstrong woman. But just how headstrong and willful she was, the world was yet to discover.

Hatshepsut and Thutmose II ascended the throne peacefully about 1520 B.C. Their reign seems to have lasted about eighteen years and to have been rather uneventful. In time two daughters were born to the royal couple. But, to her sorrow, Hatshepsut never had a son.

The only male offspring of Thutmose II, in fact, was born to a lowly harem woman named Isis. (Things get a little confused along here. Some sources say that he was really the son of Thutmose I, but no matter.) When her brother-husband died, Hatshepsut was forced to stand by while this son of a nobody ascended the throne of her sacred ancestors.

Thutmose III was a boy of only ten or twelve at the time. Such a child was easily bent to the will of his brilliant and ambitious stepmother. According to the record left by Ineni, the royal architect, the real power was soon in her hands.

"It was the god's wife, Hatshepsut, who managed the affairs of the Two Lands by reason of her own designs, and Egypt was made to labor with bowed back for her, the excellent seed of the god—who satisfies the two regions when she speaks."

So it went for seven years. Then the queen apparently

had enough of playing second fiddle to a monotonous string of Thutmose. She enlisted the suport of Hapuseneb, vizer and high priest of the great god Amon, and Senmut, chief steward of the god's estates. With the backing of that powerful priesthood, it was all too easy.

Hatshepsut simply tied the ceremonial lion's tail about her slender waist. She adorned her chin with the symbolic golden beard. She placed the red and white double crown of Upper and Lower Egypt upon her own small head, the golden serpent upon her brow. In short, she took over the regalia as well as the power of the throne.

Behold! The queen had become pharaoh!

If there were those among her courtiers who failed to take this astonishing transformation seriously, they were soon made aware of their error. Hatshepsut was hailed on every hand as the female Horus, sacred hawk god of Egypt. Every convention of temple and court had to be twisted to fit the sex of the new pharaoh. Even the terms for addressing a sovereign had to be put into feminine form. There might not have been a word for her, but there was no doubt that she *was* pharoah.

Thutmose was graciously allowed to retain the empty title of co-regent. Actually, he was reduced to a mere puppet. He was forced into a marriage with Hatshepsut's daughter, Neferu Re. It is to be doubted, in fact, that the unfortunate young man retained control of even his own household.

He could expect no support from the priests. They were solidly behind the queen. And, while the nobles may have been shocked, they all believed Hatshepsut to be the only true descendant of the ancient gods. As for the common people, a clever propaganda campaign took care of public opinion. Everywhere scenes were carved and painted reminding the people that Hatshepsut had long ago been declared heir to the throne by her father. Everywhere the great king was shown with hands outstretched as he called upon the gods to witness his public acknowledgment of that fact.

And everywhere the people accepted this strange turn of events with hardly a murmur. Hatshepsut could proceed with the business of ruling without fear of a counter-revolution to shake her from the throne.

Actually, there was no real change. Hatshepsut had already shown herself to be a capable administrator. The policies of Thutmose III had long been her policies. His laws were her laws; his commands were her commands. Only now the official business of the realm was transacted in her name. No one stood between her and the full glory of kingship.

It was a heady feeling!

Perhaps Thutmose expected the ancient gods of Egypt to punish his wicked stepmother for her crimes. He had been chosen as king. He had worn the double crown. He had been hailed as the reincarnation of the sun god Amon Ra. The heavens should cry at this outrage.

If he had such thoughts, he was due for much disappointment. On the contrary, the gods seemed to smile on Hatshepsut's unorthodox reign. And Egypt was apparently none the worse for having a female pharaoh on the throne. Actually, the times favored the experiment.

The highly successful military campaigns of her father, grandfather, and husband had consolidated the empire and demoralized all would-be enemies. Thus Egypt's frontiers were safe from invasion and her revenues secure. Hatshepsut could boast without fear of contradiction, "My eastern boundary is as far as the marshes of Asia; my western boundary is as far as the sunset!"

Nor had the common people any real cause for complaint. The wretched serfs who eked out a bare living from the soil or labored on the great building projects were no worse off under a woman ruler. The craftsmen and merchants were well satisfied. Peace and an unending flow of tribute from distant lands meant good times and booming trade.

There was no need for Hatshepsut to expose her feminine frailty on the field of battle. She need not risk her person or her throne in the hazards of war. It was only necessary that she maintain a strong grip on the scepter, evade the ever-present danger of a palace revolution, and keep peace among her subjects. In these she seems to have been notably successful.

Still, a pharaoh must have some momentous event to immortalize in statues and inscriptions—some glorious deed to record on the walls of his tomb. Hatshepsut devoted much time and wealth to restoring the monuments of her ancestors which had fallen into disrepair. But she was also building a magnificent funerary temple for herself. Her architects and master builders labored steadily, planning and erecting memorials to the everlasting glory of their queen. With literally acres of wall space to fill with the customary murals and reliefs, Hatshepsut needed some outstanding achievement to commemorate.

Perhaps that is why she sent the celebrated expedition to Punt.

One day as the queen stood before the shrine of Amon, "a command was heard from the great throne, an oracle of the god himself, that the ways of Punt be searched out, that the highways to the myrrh trees should be penetrated."

It was in the ninth year of her reign, she tells us, that she conceived the plan of creating a garden of myrrh trees and dedicating it to the glory of Amon. But such trees grew only in a mysterious, faraway land. No one had been there in a long, long time. Nevertheless, Hatshepsut equipped a fleet of five ships and sent it off down the east coast of Africa. Its goal was a fabulous land which has never yet been satisfactorily identified.

In due time, the ships returned. They were heavily laden with "marvels of the country of Punt; all goodly fragrant woods of god's land, heaps of myrrh resin, of fresh myrrh trees, with ebony and pure ivory, with green gold of Emu, with cinnamon wood, with incense, eye cosmetic, with baboons, monkeys, dogs, with skins of the southern panther, with natives and their children." Verily, in the words of the chronicler, "never was the like of this brought for any king who has been since the beginning!"

The delighted queen shared her rich booty with Amon. We are told that she offered the god a live panther and piles of gold and myrrh twice as tall as a man, among other gifts, and of course the thirty-nine living myrrh trees she had promised for his garden.

The queen wanted something very special to mark the

thirtieth anniversary of her appointment to the succession. She ordered that two great obelisks "of electrum (a gold-and-silver alloy) whose points mingled with heaven" be set up. The shafts of granite had to be cut at the quarries near the First Cataract and floated down to Thebes on barges. The stupendous difficulty of such a task is apparent when we know that each obelisk was nearly one hundred feet long and weighed roughly three hundred and fifty tons.

For some reason, the queen chose to erect these monsters in the colonnaded hall of the temple at Karnak. This required that portions of the great structure her father had built be destroyed. Once in place, they towered incredibly high over the temple—so high, in fact, that Hatshepsut felt called upon to swear a lengthy and solemn oath that each was carved from a single block of stone. The precious alloy with which the tips were covered was measured out by the queen's own hand. It took twelve *bushels* in all.

Lesser obelisks and temples no less lavishly adorned marked other events of the reign. The crowning achievement of Hatshepsut's vast building projects, however, was the funerary temple which nestled against the western cliffs of the Nile Valley at Deir el-Bahri. It is universally hailed as one of the most beautiful monuments in Egypt—in all the world, for that matter. Impressively lovely even in ruins, it must have been truly breathtaking when Hatshepsut was alive to supervise the details of its completion.

How proud she must have been on the day that the great god Amon paid his first visit to the new shrine. Surely the queen followed close behind the golden boat that bore the sacred image on its yearly pilgrimage. Stepping from her state barge, her first sight would have been the tree-lined avenue which stretched some three miles inland from the river bank. Spaced at close intervals on either hand, pairs of brightly painted sandstone sphinxes guarded the approach to the temple. Each had the body of a lion but a human head. The features were those of Hatshepsut.

But now the procession moved on. The glittering bark of the god was almost hidden by clouds of perfumed smoke from the dozens of censers. Musicians and singers filled the air with hymns of praise. Ostrich-plume fans waved and nodded and gaily colored banners streamed in the breeze as the white-clad priests made their way slowly upward.

Up the gently sloping ramps with their carved and painted sacred snakes, past the "proto-Doric" colonnade of the second terrace went the god and his court. The covered portico of the third terrace boasted limestone pillars in the likeness of the god of the underworld, Osiris. Again, the painted features were Hatshepsut's.

From this terrace great bronze doors sealed off the inner shrine which was carved into the living rock of the cliff. As each door swung open to admit the god, the elaborately inlaid designs of electrum caught the light. Along the walls on either side every inch of space was crowded with glowing murals.

Some of these showed the miraculous birth of the great queen. Others depicted in minute detail the voyage to Punt. It may have been on this upper terrace, too, that the precious myrrh trees were planted.

"It was done," Hatstepsut told her assembled nobles.

( 23 )

"I have made for him a Punt in his garden just as he commanded me. It is large enough for him to walk abroad in it."

Such monuments continued to attest to the female pharaoh's greatness. Then, after a reign of twenty-one years, they ceased abruptly. Thutmose III was suddenly the only power in the land.

Whether assassination, a successful revolution, or simply natural death marked the end, we do not know. Certainly Thutmose was not kind to his stepmother-aunt's memory. But, under the circumstances, he can hardly be blamed. His long-repressed vengeance is hardly proof that he was responsible for her disappearance.

Nevertheless, it was with a dedicated fury that he set about erasing her name and likeness from the memory of the people. Her statues were torn down or defaced. Her inscriptions were ruthlessly hacked from walls and monuments. Even the bases of her proud obelisks were sealed off and rededicated so that none might give her credit for their erection.

Only recently has the obliterating stonework crumbled away to reveal to the world the true glory of Hatshepsut, female pharaoh and history's first important petticoat ruler.

CLEOPATRA, FROM AN EGYPTIAN
REPRESENTATION

# 2

# CLEOPATRA VII:
## Who Dreamed of World Empire

In the year 48 B.C. two armies lay encamped on the edge of the eastern desert near Pelusium. One was commanded in the name of a fifteen-year-old king by the wily and experienced Egyptian general Achillas. The other was under the sole command of an inexperienced nineteen-year-old girl.

They awaited only a signal to begin the battle. The desert would ring to the clash of arms. Men would kill and be killed. And in the end the fate of the girl would be decided.

For she was Cleopatra, seventh queen of that name, and rightful co-regent of the Egyptian Empire.

( 27 )

Her father, Ptolemy Auletes, had left his throne jointly to his two oldest children. According to ancient custom, Cleopatra and her young brother were married. They had ascended the throne as husband and wife in 52 B.C. But the boy-king was only a puppet in the hands of his evil ministers, Achillas and Pothinus. They worked incessantly against Cleopatra, whom they could not control. Three years later they succeeded in driving her from the throne.

Now she was back with an army to back up her claims. But the impending battle was never to take place.

Instead, couriers rode into both camps with some startling news. The news concerned another battle—one which had already been fought in far-off Greece. There, at Pharsala, Roman legions under Julius Caesar had met and defeated other legions under Pompey. Caesar had emerged as the undisputed master of the Roman Empire. Pompey had fled to take refuge in Egypt, only to meet a treacherous death.

Pothinus, hoping to please Caesar, had ordered him killed.

Now Caesar himself had landed at Alexandria in pursuit of his fleeing enemy. He was met by young Ptolemy and the grinning Pothinus, who presented him with Pompey's severed head!

Julius Caesar was never a vindictive foe. Pompey had once been married to his only child, and he was prepared to forgive and forget. Instead of being pleased, the great Roman was appalled and disgusted at this act of needless cruelty. Angrily, he summoned both Ptolemy and Cleopatra to appear before him and settle their quarrels.

The will of Ptolemy Auletes had given Caesar all the excuse he needed to interfere in Egyptian affairs. That will had made the two children wards of the Republic of Rome. Now, to all intents and purposes, Julius Caesar *was* the Republic of Rome.

Knowing all this, Cleopatra was more than willing to answer that summons, for Caesar was known to be just. And he had seen for himself what manner of men Ptolemy's precious advisers were. Surely he would look with favor upon her claims.

But there was just one problem.

Between her and Alexandria lay many miles of hostile territory. Should she fall into the hands of her enemies, her fate would be sealed without a doubt. Pothinus would have no qualms in having her destroyed. He could ill afford to let her reach the ear of Caesar. And even if she should reach the capital safely, there would still be danger. Every gate was sure to be closely guarded.

But Cleopatra had a plan. Not even Ptolemy's men would dare to interfere with a gift from their king to Caesar. She summoned her faithful servant, Appollodorus.

And so it happened that a small boat with muffled oars slipped silently along the delta in the dark of night. Past the tall Egyptian ships, past the proud Roman galleys it crept to tie up at last by the quay of the palace itself. Then Appollodorus effortlessly shouldered the roll of splendid, jewel-toned oriental carpet.

The "gift" passed unchallenged into the very presence of Caesar.

Imagine, then, the surprise when the glowing carpet was unrolled. From its folds the graceful form of a nineteen-year-old girl stepped forth—a girl who proudly announced herself to be none other than Cleopatra VII, rightful Queen of Egypt!

This romantic story is undoubtedly true. But the Cleopatra who survives in today's popular legends—the cruel and cunning oriental despot, the sultry enchantress of the Nile—is a fraud. Oh, she was Queen of Egypt all right. And, what is usually overlooked, she was an unusually capable ruler.

But Cleopatra was not even an Egyptian. She was a Greek, and her heritage, her education, and her own inclinations drew her and her policies into the sphere of Europe, not Asia.

This fascinating queen was a direct descendant of an ambitious Greek general named Ptolemy. He had seized Egypt for himself out of the wreck of Alexander the Great's empire some three centuries before she was born, and had founded a new dynasty. It cannot be claimed that the Ptolemies were an attractive ruling family. They soon adopted all the vices of the ancient pharoahs and added a few Greek refinements of their own devising.

Their record of bitter family rivalries for the throne is appalling. Children consistently murdered their parents, and vice versa. Brothers climbed to power over the bodies of brothers. Wives eliminated unwanted husbands by dagger or poison. As a child, Cleopatra had witnessed a bloody rebellion led by her sister, Berenice, against their father. In the end, Ptolemy Auletes had won. He then callously ordered the execution of his own daughter. The lesson was not lost on little Cleopatra.

The struggle between Cleopatra and the young Ptolemy was only one more chapter in the violent history of their house. Caesar cannot have had more than a passing interest in the squabbles of Egyptian monarchs—that is, not until the charming and intelligent young queen brought herself so dramatically to his attention. He heard and heeded Cleopatra's impassioned tale of wrongs.

When young Ptolemy swaggered in for an audience with Caesar he received quite a shock. Seated at the side of the powerful Roman was his sister-wife. The sight of his detested rival in that place of honor sent Ptolemy into a towering rage. Only the quick action of Roman guards and his own advisors kept the queen from physical assault. But they could not prevent the boy's furious curses. Finally, he threw off his own crown, trampled it underfoot, and fled from the room screeching that he had been betrayed.

Caesar succeeded in reconciling the two rulers, but the peace was short-lived. An additional complication was soon added by another sister, Arsinoë. Seizing upon the general disorder, she declared herself queen. Revolt flared through the land. Caesar and Cleopatra found themselves besieged in the palace quarter of Alexandria with only a handful of Roman soldiers for protection. Only the military genius of Caesar could save them from destruction. Even he, however, could do little but organize a masterful defense.

It was in the fierce struggle for control of the all-important harbor that the greatest loss of this so-called Alexandrian war occurred. At Caesar's command, Egyptian shipping was burned along the waterfront. The great Alexandrian library, founded by the first Ptolemy, accidently caught fire. The largest collection of books and manuscripts the world had ever known went up in flames. The magnitude of the loss is incalculable. Thousands of papyrus rolls were lost that could never be replaced.

In the end, reinforcements from Rome allowed Caesar to sally forth from the besieged palace and make short

work of his enemies. Ptolemy was killed in battle, and
Arsinoë was taken prisoner. Cleopatra, married again to
another young brother named Ptolemy, was safely established on the throne of Egypt.

In his *Bellum Alexandrinum* Caesar wrote the only direct reference he ever made to the Egyptian Queen.
"Caesar restored the Queen Cleopatra because she had always been loyal to him and had always remained with
him in headquarters." Now, it would seem, his work was
done. Why, then, did the dictator linger and not return to
Rome? Why did he continue month after month in the
exotic land of the Nile?

In truth, he had become so infatuated with Cleopatra
that he could not tear himself away. This aging general, a
battle-scarred veteran of countless campaigns, had surrendered to a girl barely out of her teens. She, in turn,
seems to have loved him sincerely as father, teacher, hero,
and savior—perhaps even as husband. For some say that
Caesar went through an Egyptian marriage ceremony with
her.

Every moment each could share from the press of official
duties was spent together. He taught her to be a true
queen, to rule with wisdom and justice. She taught him
how to relax and enjoy the fruits of his many victories. One
memorable experience they shared was a romantic voyage
up the Nile in the queen's luxurious royal barge.

The *Thalameyos* was really a floating palace. Aside from
the sumptuous apartments of the illustrious passengers, it
contained banqueting halls, a chapel to Aphrodite and
Dionysos, even a small but charming garden. The many
decks were shaded by linen awnings cleverly contrived to
protect them at any hour from the blazing Egyptian sun.

Troops of slaves—dancing girls, actors, singers, artists—were at hand. Expert cooks prepared meals on another ship fitted out as a complete kitchen. Finally, four hundred smaller vessels carried a small army of Roman soldiers.

Amidst all this splendor, Caesar allowed himself to be carried far from the prosaic world of Rome. Like any modern tourist, he was awed by the ancient glories of Egypt. It was an enchanted journey.

But there was another reason for prolonging the stay. Some time after the return to Alexandria, a son was born to Cleopatra. She called the child Ptolemy Caesar, but from the first he was known as Caesarion—little Caesar.

Rome, however, kept calling her most illustrious son back to the paths of duty. Finally, he could delay no longer. He left Egypt—and Cleopatra—for a series of lightning campaigns in Asia Minor. It was of one of these that he wrote the famous one-line report, *"Veni, vidi, vici* (I came, I saw, I conquered)."

It was a year and a half before Cleopatra saw him again.

Then Caesar used his influence as dictator to arrange a state visit to Rome by the King and Queen of Egypt. Little attention was paid to the young king, though he fell ill and died during the visit. Cleopatra, however, was quite another matter.

Caesar himself met her at the gates of Rome. Together they drove through streets packed with citizens. Everyone was eager to catch a glimpse of the foreign enchantress who, it was whispered, had cast a spell upon the great Caesar. Perhaps they understood a little better when they saw her. The young queen was dressed in dazzling cloth of silver and draped in ropes of shimmering pearls.

Much has been written to prove that Cleopatra was not

truly beautiful. Since descriptions of her are woefully incomplete and portraits virtually nonexistent, we cannot know, and it does not really matter. Certainly, none deny her exquisite grace and charm.

As the common men lined the streets to see her, so did the high-born Romans flock to her villa by the Tiber to pay their court. Caesar, of course, spent every free moment enjoying the company of his beloved and romping with little Caesarion.

Though she was not exactly loved by her hosts, Caesar saw to it that every possible public honor was paid the royal guest. The Roman populace, for instance, was startled to discover that it was a statue of Cleopatra that was enshrined in the newly dedicated temple of Venus. New coins were issued on which the images of Venus and Eros could be clearly recognized as the queen of Egypt and her small son. Nor was she denied a place on the tribune among the highest in the land when Caesar celebrated his many triumphs. During those fabulous four days she was seated not far from his Roman wife, Calpurnia.

Among the wretched prisoners who marched through the streets in chains Cleopatra saw her own sister, Arsinoë. There is no record that the queen felt the slightest twinge of pity at the sight. However, it was to have a profound effect on her later life.

Life in Rome was gay and exciting. Great plans were afoot that opened giddy vistas of world empire to Cleopatra. It seemed certain that Caesar would soon be emperor of Rome. And after that, who knew?

Such dreams were ended forever by the dreadful events of March 15, 44 B.C.

Great Caesar fell at the hands of assassins, and with him

died Cleopatra's hopes of ruling the world at his side. Even worse, Caesar's will named his nephew, Octavian, as his heir. Caesarion was not acknowledged as his son, nor even mentioned. There was nothing for the heart-broken queen to do but return to Egypt.

– She left a Rome already plunged into another bloody civil war. It was a war from which two men were to emerge as victors—Marc Antony and Octavian. In time, they divided the Roman Empire between them. Antony took the eastern half as his portion. A few years later he haughtily summoned Cleopatra to meet him at Tarsus. He wanted the Egyptian Queen to affirm her allegiance to her Roman alliance before he marched against Parthia. He got a great deal more than he bargained for.

Cleopatra came to Tarsus, all right. But she delayed her coming long enough to let the world—and Antony—know that she came of her own free will. Nor was that all.

"She came sailing up the Cydnus," wrote Plutarch, "in a barge with gilded stern and outspread sails of purple, while oars of silver beat time to the music of flutes and fifes and harps. Word went through all the multitude that Venus was come to feast with Bacchus for the good of all Asia."

The oriental splendor of her gowns, the astonishing lavishness of her entertainments dazzled Antony. But it was her own sparkling wit and "the charm of her conversation" that bewitched the simple Roman soldier. Antony promptly fell head over heels in love with this fairy-tale queen. When Cleopatra returned to Egypt, Antony, forgetting all thoughts of duty, sailed with her aboard that fabulous barge.

Once more Cleopatra had enslaved the greatest of the

Romans. Once more a Roman general went through an Egyptian marriage ceremony with a foreign queen. And once more Cleopatra herself was deeply, truly in love. But there were more important reasons than love for what she did. The old dream of world empire had begun to stir again.

Cleopatra certainly knew that Antony was but a poor imitation of Julius Caesar. Still, he loved Caesar and he hated Octavian. What she really wanted from him was aid in establishing Caesarion as Caesar's heir. And it was not in Antony's power to give her this.

Octavian's growing power soon posed a threat to Antony himself. He must return to Rome to regain the popular approval he had lost by months of dalliance at the Egyptian court. Once there, he allowed himself to be persuaded into marriage with his rival's sister. Octavia was to be the guarantee of peace between her brother and her husband. Rome breathed more freely as the threat of another civil war faded.

But the news was a bitter blow to Cleopatra. Not only were her hopes for Caesarion dashed, but she felt herself the injured wife. Especially so since she had borne twins to Antony during his absence. The boy she named Alexander Helios, the girl Cleopatra Selene.

For more than three years the abandoned queen brooded over her wrongs. How it must have galled the soul of so proud a woman that her faithless lover seemed quite content with his new wife. She was not to know that Antony had made a new and secret will on the eve of his marriage. It was his wish that after death his body should be carried to Alexandria to lie at the side of Cleopatra!

Then Antony traveled eastward once more. He arrived

in Antioch with his legions to put down revolt in Asia Minor. Once again he sent for the Queen of Egypt. Once again she came, he saw, and *she* conquered. It was as if the years with Octavia had never been.

The people of Rome were soon appalled at Antony's free-handedness—giving away their lands to form kingdoms for Caesarion and the twins. They were outraged at his flouting his marriage vows to the gentle Octavia. They were dismayed at his terrible defeat when at last he moved against the Parthian rebels. Nor did the crafty Octavian ever allow them to forget just how appalled, outraged, and dismayed they were. Every foolish mistake Antony made played directly into the hands of his rival, for Octavian aimed at nothing less than making himself sole heir to the empire which would have been Caesar's. A clash between the two most powerful Romans was inevitable.

In 33 b.c. it came. Antony decided to risk everything in one gamble. Accompanied by Cleopatra and her strong Egyptian fleet, he sailed to join his legions in Greece. Octavian prepared to meet him. He was careful to assure the Roman people that he went to fight Cleopatra only. "Antony," he sneered, "is not worthy of being named as an opponent."

No one has ever really understood why a capable soldier like Antony accepted the challenge of a sea battle. Even with Cleopatra's ships, his naval forces were inferior. Only on land could he face Octavian with superior numbers.

Whatever the reason, the fatal mistake was made. The two fleets met at last off the Greek coast. The Battle of Actium had begun.

Nor does anyone know why Cleopatra suddenly withdrew her fleet while the issue of that battle was still in doubt. But that is exactly what she did. Perhaps it is easier to understand why Antony abandoned his men and sailed after her. Easiest of all is the reason he sat in numb despair, refusing to speak to anyone throughout the long voyage. He had risked all and lost all—even his honor.

It was nearly a year before Octavian was ready to follow up his victory with an invasion of Egypt. It was a year of alternating hope and despair for Antony and Cleopatra. But the clear-eyed queen knew it was only a matter of time. She had a number of her ships dragged across the desert to the shores of the Red Sea, hoping to escape in that direction when the time came. When the ships were burned by marauding Arabs, she made other plans.

As Octavian's army approached Alexandria, Antony marched out to meet him. But the legions would no longer fight for a shamed general. Antony's fleet and troops deserted to the enemy. In despair he challenged Octavian to single combat. Octavian scorned to meet him. He had other plans for punishing traitors and cowards.

Meanwhile, Cleopatra had taken refuge with all her treasure and two of her women in her own magnificent tomb. She caused word to be spread that she had taken her own life. Hearing this, Antony fell on his own sword. Though the wound was mortal, he lingered until he heard that Cleopatra still lived. He begged to be taken to her. He was raised by ropes into the upper chamber of the tomb, for the women feared treachery should the great doors be opened.

And there, in the arms of his beloved, Antony breathed his last.

Cleopatra negotiated with Octavian from the safety of the tomb. She was lulled into a sense of false security at first by his promises of honorable treatment. Then she realized that this Roman was not only immune to her charms but that he had only one aim. Octavian would not be content until he had taken her to Rome as his prisoner.

Plans that she had made long ago were set in motion. The proud Cleopatra would never be dragged captive through the streets of Rome. She would not be chained to the wheels of a conquerer's chariot like her sister, Arsinoë.

The romantic legend of the venomous serpent concealed in a basket of figs may or may not be true. But it is certain that Octavian was cheated of his final revenge. He found his prisoner lying on her golden couch. She was dressed in the regal splendor she had worn on state occasions. The great double crown of Upper and Lower Egypt was placed on her head.

But Cleopatra was dead, and Egypt as an independent land died with her.

So, in her thirty-ninth year, the end came for Cleopatra.

Twice she had dreamed of ruling the world at the side of the man she loved, and twice she had almost seen that dream come true.

Her two faithful women followed their mistress even to the grave. When Octavian's men broke in they found Iras already dead.

"Was this well done of your lady, Charmian?" they demanded.

"Extremely well," replied the dying Charmian, "and as became the descendant of so many kings."

BOUDICCA FOUGHT FOR ANCIENT BRITAIN

# 3

# BOUDICCA:
## Conquer or Die!

A hush fell over the densely packed throng as the chariot moved slowly into view. Of the three occupants two were girls, young and fair to look upon. But it was the third, a woman past the bloom of youth, upon whom every eye was fixed.

She would have commanded respect anywhere, this woman, even without the circlet of gold which marked her rank. There was about her an air of fierce pride. Clearly she was not of humble origin. Her every gesture showed that she was accustomed to command—and to having her orders obeyed.

As indeed she was. For this was Boudicca, Queen of the Iceni! And she was the undisputed leader of this vast assortment of bronzed and bearded warriors.

Boudicca was a woman of ancient lineage. Her ancestors had ruled over the tribes of this misty island as far back as the memory could reach. She had married the reigning king of the Iceni many years ago. And yet, but for a strange twist of fate, this pagan queen might have lived out her days in obscurity.

Destiny had decreed otherwise.

Today, she could look out over a sea of Britons. Horned helmets and round leather shields tossed and glittered in the sun. Brawny arms brandished spears and lances and battle axes—even scythes—on high. The petty quarrels were forgotten. The tribes were united as never before to meet a common foe.

The strange drama of her life had pitted this woman against the might of the Roman Empire. The final act was about to begin.

"Men of Britain!" Boudicca's voice rang out.

"You see before you one whom our enemies scorn as only a weak and useless creature. You, however, well know that the women of Britain have never been weaklings. You have fought many a battle under the leadership of one of us.

"But it is not as a woman descended from noble ancestry but as one of the people that I am avenging my lost freedom, my scourged body, the outraged chastity of my daughters. Roman lust has gone so far that not even our persons, nor even age or virginity, are left unpolluted!

"But heaven is on the side of righteous vengeance. A

legion which has dared to fight has perished. The rest are hiding themselves in their camp or thinking anxiously of flight. They will not stand before even the din and the shout of so many thousands, much less our charge or our blows!"

Perhaps there was a wave of coarse laughter at this sally. But the queen's next words were sobering.

"If you weigh well the strength of the armies and the causes of this war, you will see that in this battle you must conquer or die! This," she cried, "is a woman's resolve." And she stung their pride with a final, "As for men, they may live—and be slaves!"

There was no need to say more. Every man there knew too well the heavy hand of Roman oppression. And the recent outrages under Suetonius had made life all but unbearable for many.

Prasutagus, king of the Iceni, had viewed the cruelties of the legions with growing alarm. Wherever the conquerers marched they left a trail of burning farms and mutilated bodies. Unarmed peasants could not resist. Death could be avoided only at the price of slavery, and property was ruthlessly confiscated.

Worst of all, the sacred groves were put to the torch. The ancient altars were broken and defiled. The holy and learned men of the Druidic priesthood had been driven to take refuge on the island of Mona. But even here they were not safe. Suetonius threw the strength of his legions against the sacred community, and the Druids were massacred. Not even the comfort of their religion was left to the unhappy Britons.

It was in the fond hope of averting similar disasters

from his own kingdom that Prasutagus made his plans. When death approached, he made a will leaving half his lands to the Emperor Nero. Such a token of submission, he reasoned, would absolutely insure the remaining half for his wife and daughters. He could hardly have been more mistaken.

The Roman historian Tacitus tells us what happened.

"The reverse was the result. So much so that his kingdom was plundered by centurions, his house by slaves, as if they were the spoils of war. All the chief men of the Iceni, as if Rome had received the whole country as a gift, were stripped of their ancestral possessions, and the king's relatives were made slaves."

As a crowning insult to a helpless people, the dead king's daughters were treated in the grossest possible manner. And the widowed queen was publicly scourged!

Queen Boudicca was a proud woman of uncommon intelligence and courage. The humiliations to which she and her daughters were subjected kindled within her half-savage breast a white-hot hatred of everything Roman. It is hardly surprising then to find her leading a conspiracy to destroy the oppressors.

Cautiously, she set to work to kindle the spirit of rebellion in her broken people. Secret envoys glided along the dark paths of the forest to seek the aid of neighboring kingdoms. Even tribes like the Trinovantes, who had yet to feel the heavy hand of tyranny, were summoned. All were so horrified at the events reported by Boudicca's messengers that they pledged themselves to revolt at her signal.

Meanwhile, rumors of what was happening had reached

the Roman colonists of Camulodunum. Alarming omens were reported, and frenzied women mouthed wild prophecies of impending doom. Was it only an accident that the statue of Victory in the forum fell from its pedestal in the middle of the night? Had it not turned its back on the brooding forests as if fleeing an unseen enemy?

A hasty appeal for aid was sent to the Roman governor. He dispatched two hundred men. It was a woefully inadequate force to defend an unfortified town which was already surrounded by masses of enraged natives. But perhaps there were not enough legions in all Britain to resist the pent-up fury of the attack when it came. Certainly two hundred soldiers could do nothing. Camulodunum was overrun and its entire population destroyed without mercy.

A few days later came an even greater victory. The ninth legion, on its way to relieve the city, was ambushed. Only a handful of cavalry escaped to carry the tale of disaster back to Suetonius.

Encouraged by such successes, tribe after tribe hurried to join Boudicca's swelling forces. The revolt spread like wind-whipped flames. Londinium and Verulamium were taken, and their inhabitants were put to the sword. It is estimated that between seventy and eighty thousand men, women and children lost their lives in the orgies of bloodletting which followed each victory.

Queen Boudicca's plans for vengeance had succeeded beyond her wildest dreams. Roman blood had run in torrents, which must have satisfied even her outraged pride. Roman treasures and arms were heaped in incredible profusion on the carts that followed her victorious armies.

And the eagles of the ninth legion, glittering symbols of Roman might, marched before her as trophies of war.

But the final test was yet to come, and she knew it. Suetonius, governor of Britain, had now arrived at the head of ten thousand veteran troops to put down the revolt.

The triumphant army of Britons believed that their tremendous numerical advantage would guarantee victory —so much so that they made rather a holiday affair of the battle. When the opposing forces were drawn up on either side of a large open plain, the rebel women and children were brought along to witness the defeat of the hated foreigners.

Suetonius, however, was not to be defeated by overwhelming numbers—nor even by Boudicca's stirring speeches. According to Tacitus, he had picked his ground well. "He had chosen a position approached by a narrow defile, closed in at the rear by a forest, having first ascertained that there was not a soldier of the enemy except in his front. . . ." Here he awaited the attack of the Britons across that open plain.

It was not long delayed. The masses of infantry and cavalry, "a vaster host than ever had assembled," charged headlong at the waiting legions. They were met with the firm and well ordered defense of experienced soldiers. The Romans clung stubbornly to their defensive position. This forced the Britons to fight on a narrow front where superior numbers were worse than useless. All they could do was get in one another's way. And so the attacking army bogged down and became a helplessly milling mob with neither aim nor direction.

Into the midst of this confusion, Suetonius ordered a charge. Like a keen-edged blade into soft flesh, the Roman wedge cut through the bewildered foe. Then the Roman cavalry began to close in on the flanks. The Britons broke and tried to flee. Instead, they became hopelessly entangled in the close-packed wagons bearing their women and children.

In vain did the valiant queen try to rally her shattered forces. A few moments before they had seemed invincible. Now, no power on earth could make them turn and face the awesome war machine of the Roman legion.

Indeed, an appalling number of them would never face anything again. Tacitus tells us rather smugly that eighty thousand Britons, including women and children, perished on that bloody plain. The total cost to Rome was four hundred dead and as many wounded.

Among the heaped-up corpses was that of Queen Boudicca.

No Roman sword had touched her, and she might easily have made her escape from the terrible carnage.

Instead, when the tide of battle had turned against her, she had resolutely swallowed the deadly poison in her little glass vial. Though she had expected victory, she would not survive defeat.

Thus, in A.D. 62, Queen Boudicca, heroine of Britain, fulfilled her pledged word to "conquer or die" with her people.

THEODORA, COURAGEOUS BYZANTIUM EMPRESS

# 4

# THEODORA:
## Cinderella Empress

The day was January 18, in the year A.D. 532. The scene was the council room of the imperial palace in Constantinople. The atmosphere was one of sheer panic.

Byzantium was aflame with the fires of revolt. Soon the rebels would be knocking at the very gates of the palace. What was to be done? Neither the emperor nor his ministers seemed to have thought for anything but escape.

But there was one person at that council who had other ideas. The empress had sat beside her husband and listened patiently to those who croaked of doom. Now, having heard enough, she began to speak.

"If there were left to me no safety but in flight, I would not fly," she said scornfully. "Those who have worn the crown will never survive its loss. Never will I see the day when I am not hailed as empress!"

She turned to Justinian.

"If you wish to fly, Caesar, well and good. You have the money, the ships are ready, the sea is clear; but I shall stay. For I love the old proverb that says, 'The Purple is the best winding sheet!'"

The courageous determination of his wife put heart into the quavering emperor. He ceased to think of flight, for flight without his beloved was unthinkable. Instead he gave orders for the defense of his throne. The palace would be defended, if necessary, until every man died at his post. Let the rebel hordes see what it meant to threaten the life of a Byzantine emperor!

The rebellion was crushed and the throne was saved. Once again Justinian had reason to be grateful to this empress he had picked up from the gutter . . . or so people said.

The real truth about the early life of Theodora is unknown. Her history is obscured as much by the pathetically whitewashed tales of the empress herself as by the vicious and scandalous accounts of her enemies. Not even her birthplace is known for certain. Some sources say it was Syria; others the Island of Cyprus. The year was probably A.D. 500.

She claimed that her father was of senatorial rank. It seems more likely that he was a poor man, a keeper of the bears at the Hippodrome, named Acacius. There is little doubt that the family came to Byzantium when Theodora and her sisters were still very small. She was reared among the dregs of society backstage at the great theater and arena.

In time, the beautiful young girl emerged into the limelight as a popular actress. She had a definite flair for pantomine and comedy, but she also appeared in the spectacles. Her small graceful figure, creamy complexion, and large, sparkling eyes assured her of a following both on and off stage. Intelligent and witty, Theodora's high-spirited and often highly immoral antics shocked and charmed the entire city. Her name became a household word. And meeting her on the streets while she was still in her teens was considered an unfavorable omen by the self-righteous.

Then she disappeared. For some years, Constantinople saw nothing of the notorious Theodora. Rumor whispered that she wandered penniless and forlorn throughout the East. According to one story, she finally fell under the influence of some pious Christians at Alexandria. At any rate she returned, a changed woman, mature and religious and seemingly determined to lead a better life.

Tradition has it that she was living with the utmost propriety in humble surroundings and earning a modest living by spinning when she met and captivated Justinian. Gossip, of course, hissed viciously of black magic and secret love charms used to enslave the prince. Certain it is that the jaded, forty-year-old heir to the throne fell madly in love with this little nobody. And he remained that way for the rest of his life.

The Emperor Justin, Justinian's uncle, seemed to have no objection to his nephew's choice. Not so his aunt Euphamia. She was outraged at the mere thought of such a degrading alliance. Justinian might raise his darling to patrician rank and shower her with all the treasures of the East, but he moved home to wait until after Euphamia's death in 523 before he could marry her.

Then Justin thoughtfully set aside the law which forbade marriage with a woman of low degree—or an actress. And the wedding finally took place. Thus, when Justinian was raised to the throne, Theodora was able to share his kingdom. Once more she returned to the Hippodrome to receive the cheers of the populace. Only this time they were cheering her as Augusta.

Whatever she may have been in her early days, it is certain that no hint of scandal ever touched the name of Theodora again. Perhaps she truly loved her royal husband. Perhaps she was too clever to risk wealth and power for the sake of a romantic intrigue.

For there is no doubt at all that Theodora thoroughly enjoyed being empress. She delighted in the sumptuous apartments, fabulous jewels, and magnificent gowns that were now hers. Nor did she forget that she owned them all to her physical beauty. Many hours of each day were devoted to the rituals of grooming and adorning herself. And nothing was allowed to interfere with her hours of rest.

She demanded her own court and delighted in creating new ceremonies and processions in which she might star in the best theatrical traditions. Her courtiers and servants were required to render abject homage to her majesty as well as her beatuy. And she insisted upon every token of respect due her exalted position.

It must be understood that a Byzantine empress, no matter what her origin, was always a ruler in her own right. Traditionally, each royal bride was invested with imperial robes and the status that went with them *before* her marriage. When she also held her husband enthralled she was, in fact, the greatest power in the land. So it was with Theodora.

"In the exercise of supreme power, the first act of Justinian was to divide it with the woman he loved," says the historian Gibbon. Truly, Theodora was "seated on the throne as an equal and independent colleague in the sovereignty of the empire, and an oath of allegiance was imposed on the governors of the provinces in the joint names of Justinian and Theodora."

Despite the fact that his wife's power was as great as his—perhaps greater—Justinian never begrudged it. Her name is beside his on every inscription of the reign. Her portrait adorns every triumphal memorial. The people vied in erecting statues to her honor. Ministers sought her advice on every important issue. In short, her authority was universally felt to the point where she could—and sometimes did—countermand one of the emperor's direct orders.

It would be pleasant to believe that her influence was always benevolent. Unfortunately, cupidity or personal enmities often prevailed. Theodora instigated and approved many an unjust action. Nevertheless, her grasp of politics and diplomacy was far superior to Justinian's, and her advice was usually sound.

Especially far-seeing was her understanding of the dangers in the religious schisms that were threatening to split the empire. To prevent religious persecutions, she did not hesitate to protect the so-called heretics and defy the papacy. She boldly caused the arrest of one pope and bent another mercilessly to her will. The Syrian and Egyptian churches owed their very existence to Theodora. This was a fact which the Church at Rome was not likely to forget or forgive.

It was this dedicated enmity of the Western Church which was mainly responsible for the odium which has been attached to her name. Indeed, the name itself was often changed from "Theo," meaning "God" to "Daemonodora"! It is probably to such sources that we owe the dark tales of torture and violent death in deep, secret dungeons. Swift and terrible punishment, we are told, overtook those who dared to oppose the demon Empress. There is even a story of a son, supposedly born before her marriage. When this boy learned of his exalted birth, it was whispered, he came to seek his mother. But he met death, not love, at her hands.

In truth, Theodora was probably no more cruel than her contemporaries—possibly even less so. Her more distinguished victims, at least those whose fate is a matter of record, fared rather well. They suffered only exile, not the death or dismemberment which was commonplace. This is hardly to say that Theodora was overflowing with the milk of human kindness. Some who incurred her wrath found themselves disgraced, framed by manufactured evidence. And we can safely assume that some, at least, were assassinated at her command.

On the other hand, she was responsible for many reforms. Constantinople was a city of legendary wealth and beauty. Yet, behind the facade of luxurious palaces and magnificent shrines lay another city of incredible want and poverty. Life was bleak for the poor, and the laws dealt harshly with anyone who stole so much as a crust of bread to keep his family from starving.

To these, Theodora showed herself truly a gift of God.

And she campaigned for more just laws. Justinian himself repeatedly credited the legal code which bears his name to his wife's sage counsel. Perhaps because of her own past, she was always especially interested in improving the lot of poor women. One crusade was for laws that would protect young girls from those who would exploit them for immoral purposes.

"We have set up magistrates to punish robbers and thieves," said the empress. "Are we not even more straitly bound to prosecute the robbers of honor and the thieves of chastity?"

No portrait of Theodora can be painted in sickly pastels. Only the most vivid colors can do her justice. Vibrantly alive, ruthless and ambitious, this actress-turned-empress loved and hated with all the passion of her headstrong nature. Her enemies returned her hatred in full measure. But then, so did her friends return her love. The lower classes and Justinian adored her.

Theodora died after a long and harrowing illness in the twenty-second year of her reign. There were many in the great, jeweled dung-heap of Constantinople who mourned her sincerely. But none mourned so bitterly as Justinian. Forever afterward the emperor's most binding and solemn oaths were sworn in the name of Theodora. He constantly referred to her as "the excellent, the wise, the beautiful sovereign."

And well he might.

It has been suggested that her most lasting memorial lies in the fact that, without Theodora, the once glorious reign of Justinian limped to a sad and miserable conclusion.

ELEANOR OF AQUITAINE

# 5

# ELEANOR OF AQUITAINE:
## Queen of Kings

On a hot day in June of the year 1137 two couriers pounded along the dusty roads of southern France. Each was headed for the Château l'Ombrière near Bordeaux. And each carried a vitally important message for the château's fifteen-year-old mistress, the Lady Eleanor.

One was the bearer of sad tidings. Eleanor's father, Duke William X of Aquitaine, had successfully completed his pilgrimage to the faraway Spanish shrine of St. James at Compostela. Unfortunately, he had not lived to make the return journey. He had died there on the eleventh of April, leaving Eleanor an orphan.

This fact certainly had a bearing on the dispatches borne by the second courier. These informed young Eleanor that the King of France had graciously granted her father's dying wish. King Louis VI was pleased to announce the bethrothal of the Lady Eleanor to His Royal Highness, the Dauphin of France!

Thus, in a single day, did the young girl find her life completely rearranged!

Duke William's death had left his oldest daughter sole owner of the vast Duchy of Aquitaine. Thousands of square miles of the finest vinyards and richest farms in France, bustling seaports on two coasts, prosperous manufacturing centers—all these were hers by feudal right. This slender slip of a girl may have been bowed with grief over the death of her father. But she could hardly help being aware that she was now the richest heiress in all Europe.

Louis VI was certainly aware of it. Since Eleanor was now absolute ruler of domains twice as large as the king could lay claim to, his haste in securing those estates for his son is understandable. The power and independence of the dukes of Aquitaine was legend. Though supposedly they owed allegiance to the crown, the ducal attitude was not exactly submissive.

"Who created thee count?" a king was once foolish enough to ask.

"Who created thee king?" asked the duke in return.

Even if Eleanor had been old and ugly, she would still have been a prize well worth the taking. Prince Louis Flores might consider himself doubly fortunate that she was neither. Actually, this solemn young man had been brought up with the idea that he would one day enter the

Church. But that was before the death of his elder brother. Now he was heir to the throne. Fate had thrust him into a role for which he was never suited.

He was now on his way southward to claim his bride.

It is perhaps typical of the political issues involved that King Louis felt called upon to issue a special command to the bridal party. Upon pain of death, no one was to "seize anything whatsoever in all of the duchy." How strange to think that anyone involved in so peaceful and joyful a mission should need that warning!

But Louis was no fool. He evidently considered the danger great. And he also knew that the Aquitanian nobles, if aroused, were quite capable of defending themselves and their property. In such an event, they might even forbid their duchess to marry the prince.

Prince Louis was immediately enchanted with his bride-to-be. The lovely, black-eyed Eleanor was considered one of the greatest beauties of her day. She inspired in him a deep devotion that would never really die. The vivacious and pleasure-loving duchess, in turn, was quite content with the slender, intelligent prince. It would be no trouble to allow him to adore her.

The marriage was celebrated with medieval pomp and splendor on the twenty-fifth of July. The young couple started immediately afterward for Paris. It was a leisurely journey. Pauses were made at every important château for lavish entertainments. Before the wedding, Louis had crowned Eleanor as Princess of France. At her city of Poitiers she returned the favor. From her hands Louis received the crown of a duke of Aquitaine.

Then the news came. King Louis VI had died on August 4th and the bridegroom was forced to rush away. The revolts which always accompanied a change of monarchs must be quelled at once. Eleanor did not reach Paris until five months after her wedding, but her entry was a triumphal one.

The little Duchess of Aquitaine was now Queen of France!

At first she contented herself with running the royal household. And this in itself was no mean task. A medieval castle was really a self-contained city. Since they were built primarily for defense, they were usually grim and bleak. Eleanor introduced many refinements from the more luxurious southland. Light and air entered those forbidding walls wherever the queen went.

She also supervised the education of children of the nobility. They were, by tradition, placed in her care. Eleanor made it her special duty to instruct the young people in the "practice of courtesy." It was a subject in which she was adept. The court at Aquitaine had long been a breeding place for romantic notions of chivalry and the first of that celebrated group of romantic poets known as troubadors.

Still, Eleanor had long been accustomed to wielding great power. With Louis' great love she was assured that her influence would be felt if she chose to meddle in affairs of state. Eleanor chose to do just that.

She urged Louis to seize the county of Toulouse, to which she had a questionable claim. Her father had been born there, and her grandmother had once owned it. Louis did not refuse her. But the nobles of France were hardly anxious to see the crown lands increased. They refused their aid, and the venture was doomed to failure. Eleanor never forgave Count Thibaut of Champagne. She held him solely responsible for her humiliation.

Her hatred led to an invasion of the count's domains—and an even worse disaster. At Vitry, Louis' unruly mercenaries viciously set fire to a church in which old men, women, and children had taken refuge. The king tried to stop the horror, but in vain. More than a thousand helpless people perished in the flames. The cries of the dying echoed in the king's conscience for the rest of his life.

To assuage that conscience, Louis conceived the idea of a second crusade. The Christian kingdoms of the Holy Land were being pressed by the infidel. The idea was enthusiastically accepted. Saint Bernard's fiery sermons aroused such fervor in his hearers that he was forced to rip up his robes to provide crosses. Louis was the first to take the cross. But Eleanor was second. She had no intention of being left behind on so exciting a venture.

Moreover, she recruited a troop of distinguished noblewomen to wear the dashing uniform she designed. Loose white tunics emblazoned with scarlet crosses, broad leather belts from which short swords dangled, and red boots with flaring, yellow-lined tops identified these female crusaders. They soon became known as the "Queen's Amazons."

One hundred thousand strong, the French crusaders set out on June 14, 1147. Their path was beset with danger and hardship, but such things seldom touched the royal encampments. Queen Eleanor had brought her maids, her stewards, and her cooks, as well as her favorite troubadors for entertainment.

Though the Byzantine emperor was appalled to see another warlike horde of Franks storming across his lands, he entertained the French monarchs lavishly. Eleanor was enchanted by the incredible luxury of this Eastern Empire. She danced and flirted until her giddy behavior aroused a storm of gossip. Louis hastily made plans to push on toward the Holy Land.

He had hoped to join forces with the German Emperor who had gone ahead. Contact was made, but only a pitiful remnant of Conrad's mighty army had survived a crushing defeat by the Turks. Louis chose another route and won a smashing victory on the way to Ephesus. But alas, he fell into an ambush at Mt. Cadmus from which he barely escaped with his life.

Much of the blame for this disaster was fixed upon Eleanor. It was said that she had persuaded the advance guard to disobey orders and leave the main army, which caused them to be cut to pieces in the mountain passes. And all because she wanted to camp out in comfort! Historians, however, doubt that the queen was responsible.

Whatever the reason, most of the proud French army had perished miserably before they reached Antioch. There, Eleanor's uncle was prince, and the royal party was warmly welcomed. Too warmly, some said. Tongues were soon wagging about the queen and her handsome kinsman. It hardly served to silence such gossip that Eleanor flatly refused to accompany her husband to Jerusalem. Louis' solution was virtually to kidnap his queen and force her to go. This was an indignity Eleanor would never forget or forgive. She determined to divorce Louis.

But first she was forced to fume for a year in Jerusalem.

When the French finally sailed for home in 1149, the king and queen traveled in separate vessels.

Eleanor allowed herself to be talked out of divorce by the pope—but not for long. Actually, the French people applauded the idea. They were scandalized by her reportedly wanton behavior in the Holy Land. Besides, in thirteen years of marriage, she had produced only two children, both of them girls. France needed an heir.

They need not have worried. Eleanor did not forget.

The queen was twenty-eight years old and still a lovely and desirable woman when she first met Henry Plantagenet, Duke of Normandy. The land-hungry duke was eleven years her junior, and whether he found her vast duchy even more desirable we will never know.

The divorce was granted in March, 1152. The grounds were polite—Louis and Eleanor were declared too closely related by blood to be legally married. Most important, Aquitaine had to be formally returned to Eleanor's control. She left immediately to claim her duchy.

The dangers for such an heiress were manifold. Twice on this one trip she barely escaped ambushes set for her. Had she been taken, she would have been held captive until she agreed to give her hand and her lands to the kidnapper. But Eleanor reached Poitiers safely.

A month later she and Henry of Normandy were wed.

Between them these newlyweds laid claim to Normandy, Le Maine, Touraine, Brittany, and Aquitaine—almost the entire western half of the continent. And, when Stephen of England died, Henry inherited the British throne as well. In December, 1154, they were crowned King and Queen of England at Westminster Abbey. Truly it was said of Eleanor that she divorced a kingdom to marry an empire!

She now settled down to produce heirs to all those titles and estates. The first son died in infancy. But four more boys—three of whom would wear the crown—and two girls appeared with astonishing regularity. Nor was childbearing her only occupation. Time after time Henry left England under her capable regency while he pursued his endless wars on the continent. Or else he left her to govern one of the French possessions while he ruled England. Her own duchy never willingly obeyed anyone other than its rightful duchess.

As the years passed, however, and Eleanor's great beauty began to fade and her usefulness to him diminished, Henry callously ignored her for younger women. In thus insulting his wife, Henry made a mistake. He reckoned without her pride and her influence. History has exonerated her of one charge current at the time. She did not poison the rival known as the "Fair Rosamonde." Eleanor was not given to petty vengeance.

Instead, she poisoned the minds of Henry's sons against him. It could not have been very difficult. Henry, an able king and ruler, was not successful as a father. He ruled his family and his possessions with an iron hand. And he was guilty of maniacal rages in which he writhed on the floor and chewed the rushes. Such a man was easy enough to hate.

Eleanor stirred that hatred to rebellion. She enlisted foreign allies, including her ex-husband, in their cause. Though she was now fifty-two, she was on her way to join the rebels when she was caught by Henry's men. She was disguised as a youth.

For eight long years the Queen of England remained a prisoner while husband and sons snarled and snapped at one another in endless warfare. Prince Henry died begging his father to release his mother. She was at last allowed to leave her prison, but not England. She was also present at the council of November, 1184, when Henry did his best to reconcile the bitter quarrels of his three remaining sons—Richard, Geoffrey, and John. The semi-united family even had Christmas together at Windsor that year.

Eleanor was now allowed to take over her duchy for a while. But Henry, apparently galled to see her so independent, removed her. In April, 1186, she was brought back and imprisoned once more.

Geoffrey was killed in a tournament that same year. He left an infant son as his heir. The struggle for the custody of little Arthur touched off another war with France. Louis was dead, and his son Philip was a more formidable enemy. Richard sided with him against his father. Henry was badly defeated and forced to offer unconditional surrender. The final blow came when he read the name of John, his favorite, on the list of those who had fought against him. Henry died muttering, "Shame, shame on a beaten king."

Eleanor had her revenge.

Richard was now king. One of his first orders was for the release of his mother. Overnight Eleanor rose from a helpless captive to Queen Regent of England.

The following years were extremely busy ones. She

made royal progress throughout the land accepting the homage of the barons in her own name as well as Richard's. She collected tremendous sums of money to finance Richard's proposed Crusade. She selected a wife for him and escorted the girl to Sicily for the wedding. She stopped in Rome on her way back to confer with the pope.

Only then could she settle down to the relatively easy task of governing the continental possessions during Richard's absence in the Holy Land. She was now nearly seventy years of age. But a contemporary chronicler, Richard Devises, could still write of her in glowing terms. She was "even now unwearied at any task and provoking wonder at her stamina—an incomparable woman; beautiful, gracious, strong-willed—yet kind."

But all was not peaceful in Richard's realm. In 1192 an alarmed Eleanor hurried across the Channel. She was just in time to prevent John from treacherously selling his brother's kingdom to France. She put an end to that nonsense by threatening to seize John's continental estates. She then took over the regency of England.

She was still there when the dreadful news reached her. Richard had been captured on his return from the Crusade and was being held for ransom in Germany.

John seized the opportunity to rebel again. He invited the French king to take over England. Eleanor promptly seized all of John's castles and mustered the home guard against the threatened invasion. Frustrated by his mother's determination, John desisted. He even, albeit grudgingly, contributed his share of the huge ransom demanded for Richard's release.

The tremendous task of negotiating the terms and

raising the ransom fell to Eleanor. She was seventy-two when she carried the money to Germany in 1194. It was a terrible mid-winter journey. But she would not, could not, trust anyone else with so important a mission.

Back in England, she saw Richard crowned once more as king. She also brought a reconciliation between Richard and John. Then she settled back to enjoy a well-earned rest.

Alas, it was not to be.

Richard was killed while besieging a castle in 1199. The heartbroken mother must hurry to France to do homage for her lands and save them for John. To seal the peace treaty she negotiated, she went to Spain. There she arranged her granddaughter's marriage to the young King of France. Then she escorted the bride back for the wedding.

Once again the weary queen sought retirement. Once again she was denied it.

At Easter in 1201 alarming rumors reached her. Trouble was brewing for John. She roused herself to travel throughout her lands and insure loyalty of dubious barons. She also wrote warning letters to John which he blithely ignored.

By 1202 her worst fears had come to pass. Eleanor fled to Poitiers, a French army at her heels. Ironically, it was led by her grandson, Arthur of Brittany. She took refuge at Mirabeau, but town and castle soon fell before Arthur's besieging army. Undaunted, Eleanor shut herself up in the keep. With only a handful of knights this eighty-year-old queen continued to hold out.

Her daring defense roused John at last. He made a desperate eighty-mile march to surprise the besiegers. Arthur was captured and Eleanor was rescued. It was one of John's few triumphs on French soil. In spite of her efforts, Eleanor would live to see the continental possessions stripped away one by one.

It cannot have made the proud queen's deathbed any easier to learn that John had lost even Castle Gaillard. This had been Richard's pride and joy. It was considered impregnable. Worst of all it was the key to the defenses of Normandy.

But Eleanor could do no more. The woman whose beauty and wit had dominated the European scene for three quarters of a century was dying.

The end came on April 1, 1204, when she was eighty-two. She was buried with due honors at Fontevrault beside her husband, Henry II, and her son, Richard I.

Even in death, Eleanor of Aquitaine was surrounded by kings.

MARGARET UNITED SCANDINAVIA

# 6

# MARGARET:
## Who United Scandinavia

On the face of it, what Margaret Valdemarsdatter accomplished was impossible.

Centuries of Christianity had done little to tame the fierce spirit of the Northmen. Their social and political structures were still firmly rooted in the old Viking traditions. And those traditions made it unthinkable that a race of warriors should submit to the rule of a weak woman.

So much so that the Princess of Denmark was not even dignified with the title of queen when she married Haakon, King of Norway. Norwegian laws forbade it.

That was in 1363, when Margaret was only ten years

old. Three years later she was sent to her husband's court to be educated. In time, the political alliance became a marriage in fact. And the year she was seventeen, two events of major importance changed everything.

Her only child, Olaf, was born, heir apparent to two thrones. And her father, Valdemar, King of the Goths, died. Margaret, who was only a king's consort in Norway, was suddenly a power to be reckoned with. In Olaf's name, she took over the throne of Denmark as queen regent.

It was immediately evident that the young queen possessed a rare genius for ruling. She knew how to use and value her newfound wealth and power. Despite her exalted rank, she could well remember the time when she had neither. A letter written to her royal husband in 1370 makes this abundantly clear.

In it, Margaret states flatly that she and her servants "suffer and are in dire need for lack of food and drink." And she goes on to beg Haakon to send her money and supplies so that "those who are with me shall not leave me on account of hunger!"

Even the Norwegians must have been impressed with Margaret's political abilities. When Haakon died in 1370, they still could not bring themselves to go so far as to make her regent for her son. But they did give her complete control of Norway's foreign affairs.

Nor did Margaret disappoint them. She used her double power wisely. One of her greatest accomplishments was the breaking up of trade monoplies of the mighty merchant princes of the Hanseatic League. She ended the economic stranglehold they had held for so long on the

Baltic people. And all Scandinavia profited from the fresh air of free enterprise.

Margaret did not fail to profit from the respect she gained. Her next step was to take advantage of the political strife which convulsed neighboring Sweden. By siding with them against their unpopular king, she was able to bind many of the most powerful Swedish nobles to her. In this she was so successful that, when Olaf came of age, she could have him declared "rightful heir to Sweden."

But now disaster struck. Just when control of the three kingdoms seemed almost within her grasp, Olaf suddenly fell ill and died.

The death of her son might easily have sounded the knell for Margaret's hopes and ambitions. She herself had no legal right to any of the thrones. But she was not a woman easily set aside. She had made herself so indispensable that unusual and unexpected things began to happen.

Perhaps it was not strange for the Danes to choose their own princess as their "rightful heir and ruler." They had no suitable male for the post. And besides, they made it clear that it was only temporary. But it *was* surprising that the Norwegians should follow suit. In 1388 they solemnly elected Margaret as the "mighty Lady and Rightful Ruler" of their kingdom. They even went the Danes one better by giving her the title for "all her living days." The Swedish nobles then hastened to do likewise.

Within six months this woman, once despised, had become the recognized sovereign of three powerful kingdoms! Four, if you count Finland, which was then a Swedish possession.

Of course, there were some problems. Albrecht of Sweden had rather fancied that *he* was king of that land. Naturally, he was resentful when Margaret was hailed as queen. The matter was settled forever in 1389 by the battle of Kalköping. There, "God gave an unexpected victory into the hands of a woman," and Albrecht wound up as her prisoner.

Margaret now held undisputed sway over the largest monarchy in all Europe. But there was still a problem. The threefold queen had no heir.

To remedy this, she adopted her grand-nephew, Eric of Pomerania. So, in 1389, the seven-year-old boy was proclaimed King of Norway. He was elected to the Swedish and Danish thrones in 1396.

Meanwhile, Margaret worked tirelessly to consolidate her gains. She increased her own power by curtailing that of her arrogant nobles. She reclaimed crown lands for the throne and forced the destruction of many a baronial stronghold. The highest offices of the land were often deliberately left vacant. The queen could thus gather their authority and privileges to herself. Above all, it was Margaret alone who dispensed the justice of the land.

But Margaret cherished one dream above all others. Much of her enormous talent and energy was bent toward achieving this great diplomatic triumph. And in June of 1397 she saw those efforts crowned with success.

That was when, in an impressively solemn ceremony, young Eric was crowned simultaneously King of Denmark, Sweden, and Norway. Thus symbolically the three separate kingdoms were united into a single realm. The Kalmar Union, as it was called, was affirmed by a binding treaty.

Unfortunately, that treaty was never legally ratified by the governments concerned.

Margaret, however, cared little for such technicalities. Even though her cherished union was in effect no more than a dynastic settlement, it conferred the one great blessing she sought. It assured peace, and the queen was satisfied.

Nominally, Margaret was now queen of lands of equal standing. In reality, her native Denmark held a position of supremacy. Swedish fiefs were turned over to loyal Danes whom she felt she could trust. Offices of state in both Norway and Sweden were often filled by Danes, or even Germans. She frequently sought the approval of the Danish Council for her acts. But the Swedes were seldom consulted and the Norwegians almost never.

Such a policy of rank favoritism weakened the national governments. It also rode roughshod over national pride. In ignoring the feelings of two thirds of her people, Margaret was making one of her few mistakes.

But the consequences of that mistake were not apparent during the queen's lifetime. It had been understood, of course, that Margaret would retire from power as soon as Eric came of age. It is nevertheless hardly surprising to discover that she did nothing of the kind. She was to keep the reins of government firmly in her own hands until her death. She could hardly have done so without at least the tacit consent of those she governed.

Indeed, her refusal to yield to Eric was not without reason, for he had early proved himself likable but weak. Margaret tried hard to teach her heir the family business. She bought the province of Gotland outright from the

Teutonic Knights in 1408. Eric was made governor of the new possession, but he had no talent for ruling. He was rash, obstinate, and given to violence. In later years he often failed miserably in projects where his aunt would have succeeded brilliantly.

Margaret, by contrast, was patient and far-seeing. Her foreign policies especially were always shrewd and statesmanlike. Her domestic policies were only slightly less so. Deeply religious, she was never intolerant of those who did not share her faith. Nor did she make the mistake of allowing the church to seize state property or to interfere in any way with her administration.

In truth, Margaret's reputation for wisdom and beauty seems to have been amply deserved. In gaining her own way, she appears to have used a combination of keen intellectualism and feminine wiles. It was the same combination used so successfully by Elizabeth of England, with whom she has been favorably compared.

In October of 1412 this amazing woman was aboard her ship in Flensburg Harbor. Margaret was nearing sixty, but still very much the queen. She was then waging a war to regain control of the Duchy of Schleswig and she had just received the homage of the city.

It was her last triumph.

The plague which was raging in the surrendered city was no respecter of rank. It leaped across the waters to strike down the great queen. Margaret fell victim to the terrible disease that had laid waste to entire cities. She died on October 28.

The dynasty Margaret Valdemarsdatter had founded remained in power for a century and a quarter. The record of Eric and his descendants brought little credit to her name. However, the union she achieved against such great odds was destined to last a long time. Denmark and Norway did not dissolve their ties until 1814.

For 434 years that union would stand as a memorial to a courageous and able queen.

Margaret had proved to all Scandinavia that women are not necessarily weak and useless creatures. She had shown herself a true and worthy descendant of the proud Viking kings from whom she sprang.

QUEEN ISABELLA OF CASTILE

# 7

# ISABELLA OF CASTILE:
## Who Brought Glory to Spain

The little princess who was born at Madrigal on April
22, 1451, could lay claim to many an illustrious ancestor.
Famous rulers like Alfred the Great of England, William
the Conqueror of Normandy, and Saint Louis of France
were among her forbears. It was soon apparent that the
young Isabella had inherited many of the qualities that
made them great.

Unfortunately, there was little likelihood that she would
ever be called upon to put those qualities to use. An older

half-brother and a younger brother stood between Isabella and the throne of her father, John II. The princess was not even educated as a possible ruler. She was taught only the social and domestic skills considered necessary to noble-women in the fifteenth century. Most important of all was the intense religious training she received.

King John died when Isabella was only four. Her half-brother ascended the throne as Henry IV. To Henry, his young sister represented little more than a valuable asset in the game of political alliances. Many a royal swain unsuccessfully sought her hand in marriage. Among them was Prince Ferdinand, heir to the neighboring kingdom of Aragon.

But Henry decided to bestow his sister, not upon some foreign prince, but upon one of his own subjects. Incredibly, he chose his boon companion, a middle-aged reprobate whose reputation was an offense to all decent people. Isabella, of course, was not consulted.

When she learned of her brother's plans, this meek young girl fearlessly defied him. But she could not stand against Henry's threats of force. She had to agree, but secretly she determined that she would never become the wife of such a man. Rather than do so, she was prepared to take her own life.

Fortunately, such a sacrifice was not demanded of her. The would-be bridegroom died on the eve of his departure to claim his royal prize.

Henry's behavior in this matter gives us a clue to his character. His management of affairs of state was no less selfish and disastrous. Revolt flared among his nobles, and a bloody civil war threatened. Since her younger brother was now dead, the disaffected nobles turned to Isabella. She was urged to join them and seize the throne.

Isabella refused. As long as Henry lived, she told them, "none other has a right to the crown." Instead, she offered to attempt a reconciliation between the warring parties. In this she was successful, though one of the terms must have been extremely galling to the king. He was forced to recognize Isabella as his only legitimate heir.

Naturally, her suitors became even more numerous and more vociferous. They were also considerably higher in rank. Matches were proposed by the King of Portugal and princes of France and England. But Isabella decided this time to choose her own husband. Her choice fell on the once-rejected Ferdinand of Aragon—a choice which was not pleasing to Henry.

Once more Isabella defied her king and brother. The marriage contract was signed without either Henry's knowledge or consent. Again Henry raged and threatened. He even sent his troops to take his rebellious sister prisoner. But Isabella was no longer alone and helpless. She fled to the city of Valladolid, which was loyal to her, not Henry.

Isabella was eighteen at this time, and considered quite beautiful. Ferdinand was a year younger and, by all accounts, handsome and well formed. Theirs is one of the truly romantic stories in the annals of history—so romantic, in fact, that one tends to forget that this was not the love story of a simple boy and girl. It was a political alliance of the utmost importance.

Isabella was safe enough at Valladolid but she dared not risk trying to cross the border into Aragon. Nor could

Ferdinand come openly to fetch his bride. Instead, he entered Castile disguised as a mule driver in a caravan of merchants. The merchants, of course, were none other than the prince's attendants.

The ruse was successful. On October 11, 1469, the two whose names will be linked forever met each other for the first time. Apparently they were pleased with one another, for on December 19 the heirs to the thrones of Aragon and Castile became man and wife.

Once they were wed, Henry could do nothing, except, of course, make life as miserable as possible for the young couple. This he did with vigor and determination. His most effective weapon was financial. He refused to allow Isabella the revenues from her lands. In consequence, the two were obliged to maintain their small court on borrowed sums and live on the ragged edge of poverty. In the end, he even tried to break his pledged word and place his own daughter on the throne.

But when Henry died four years later, the nobles declared unhesitatingly for Isabella. On December 13, 1474, she rode through the streets of Segovia on a spirited white steed. There, in the great public square, a magnificent throne had been set up. Before cheering masses of her people Isabella received the crown of Castile.

Ferdinand was not there. He was away, helping his father put down a rebellion in Aragon at the time. Nor would he have shared in his wife's coronation. Their marriage contract had carefully specified that each should rule his own inheritance without interference from the other. Still, he must have felt that Isabella would turn the realm over to him when the time came. He seems to have resented her elevation to the throne.

It was not among the new queen's smallest accomplishments that she was able to soothe her husband's wounded pride. She promised that their interests would always remain inseparable. She kept her word. All state papers carried both their signatures, and the coins of the realm bore both likenesses. Their motto remained always, "The one as much as the other."

Nevertheless, it was Isabella who ruled Castile. Hers was no easy task. The inept bungling of her brother had plunged the kingdom to a low state. The treasury was all but empty. The currency was debased. The royal courts reeked with corruption. The land was ravaged by incessant warfare, and trade was at a standstill.

Little could be done to remedy all this until the claims of Henry's daughter had been settled. She had sought the help of the King of Portugal, and war broke out between the two countries. Ferdinand led the armies of Castile and led them well. He defeated the Portuguese soundly in the Battle of Toro in 1479. Then he followed up his brilliant victory by retaking Zamora.

It was that same year that he inherited his own kingdom.

The queen was at last free to initiate the elaborate reforms she felt were necessary. New and impartial laws were proclaimed—and rigidly enforced. The privileges so long enjoyed by the nobility were sharply curtailed. Religious and military orders were forced to rid themselves of corruption. They were also required to give up the crown prerogatives they had usurped. The coinage was stabilized, and—wonder of wonders—government debts were paid promptly.

In addition, Isabella saw to it that the life-giving commerce was encouraged. The all-important merchant navy received the protection it needed. The farmer's fields were made safe from invasion.

In the short space of twenty-two years, Isabella lifted the land from the depths to which generations of misrule had plunged it. She made it strong and secure, powerful and wealthy. Needless to say, the morals of the court—and of society in general—underwent a decided change for the better. For Isabella was, above all things, an extremely pious woman.

It was, in fact, misguided religious zeal which led this most Catholic of queens into her despicable actions. Two deeds appear as dark blots on an otherwise brilliant record. For Isabella was much under the influence of her priests. And one of the most influential was her one-time confessor, the infamous Torquemada.

At his insistence, she approved the cruel and disastrous expulsion of the Jews from Spain. This was disastrous for her as well, for it deprived her land of its artists and craftsmen and depopulated its wealthiest sections. The Turkish sultan willingly took the exiles in. He simply could not understand a sovereign who could so impoverish his own kingdom "to enrich another's."

But persecution of the Jews was common in the Middle Ages. It was the second act to which Torquemada persuaded her which blackened Isabella's name for all time.

Calling on Christianity, she allowed the Inquisition to take root and flourish on Spanish soil.

Within one year of the establishment of the dreaded Holy Office, two thousand martyrs had perished in its flames in Andalusia alone. Seventeen thousand more are estimated to have been deprived of property and civil liberties. And the fiendish tortures to which the unfortunate victims were subjected made the "Spanish Inquisition" a phrase to strike terror into every soul. It remains a byword even today.

Religious fanaticism was also the motivating force of the long wars against the Moors. For centures these Arab Moslems had held undisputed sway in Spain. They had made it a center of culture and learning. For centuries more they had been pushed back step by step until they retained only a small area in the south. Now Ferdinand and Isabella determined to drive them out of Europe entirely.

For ten long years, beginning in 1481, Isabella labored to recruit and supply her armies for this "Holy War." Ferdinand commanded the troops and directed the campaigns. But it was the frequent presence of their queen in the front line which inspired the men to victory. When a setback was suffered or morale dropped, Isabella had only to make an appearance, and the army took heart again. They loved the sight of her, wearing full armor, mounted on a noble steed. And the Moors were convinced that an army led by so heroic a figure would never give up.

During the final siege of Granada, fire accidentally

destroyed the Spanish camp. Isabella ordered that a permanent city be built in its place. The soldiers wanted to name the new city Isabella, but the queen insisted that it be called Santa Fe as a symbol of her faith. She and Ferdinand now took up residence at the front. And there they stayed until this last of the Moorish strongholds fell in April, 1492.

There too Isabella received once again the Genoese mapmaker who had been cooling his heels at her court for years. He was awaiting a decision on a certain venture he had proposed. He had cleverly baited Ferdinand with the promise of untold wealth. For Isabella the lure was many heathen souls to be won for Christ. Still, the final answer was a regretful "No."

Christopher Columbus departed the court in anger. He was on his way to offer his plan of discovery to France when he was stopped at the border by a messenger from the queen. Isabella had despaired of trying to persuade Ferdinand to the scheme. She had decided to attempt it on her own.

"I will assume the undertaking for my own crown of Castile," she told Columbus, "and I am ready to pawn my jewels to defray the expenses of it, if the funds in the treasury shall be found inadequate."

Popular belief to the contrary, no such sacrifice was necessary. Isabella kept her jewels. The expedition was equipped and dispatched, and the results are history. The discovery of the New World, however, brought many new problems to the queen. Not the least of them was the discoverer himself.

Columbus had demanded and received many honors and powers. But he soon proved himself proud, jealous, and totally unfit to govern. Nevertheless, the queen remained his staunch friend and supporter. She even diverted the funds earmarked for her son's wedding to finance the great navigator's third voyage of discovery. The trials and disappointments of the admiral's last years were not of Isabella's making.

The administration of the new colonies imposed a heavy burden on a woman already bowed with grief. Isabella was not fortunate in her children. Prince John, her only son, died in 1497. His death was closely followed by that of the eldest daughter, Isabella, Queen of Portugal, whose son died in infancy.

In time, Isabella's heart was gladdened by the birth of another grandson. This child of her second daughter, Joanna, was destined to grow up to be Emperor Charles V. He would inherit his grandmother's fabulous realm. Unfortunately, Joanna had already begun to show signs of the madness which would completely unbalance her. By 1503 the nobles were urging Isabella to set aside Joanna's claim to the throne.

This the queen could not bring herself to do, though her own health was failing. She became so ill that she was forced to remain on her couch. But she still supervised every detail of the business of her kingdom. In October, 1504, she executed her will.

It was a wise and memorable document. Joanna remained her heir, but with the provision that Ferdinand take over as regent should their daughter's madness persist. Her successors were solemnly bound to look after her people as she herself had always done. Not even the lowliest member of her household was forgotten in the long list of individual bequests.

Three weeks later, the queen made some changes. She had heard some ugly stories of the persecution of the helpless natives of the New World. She added a codicil designed to put an end to such abuses. It was her last official act. It is most fitting that it should have been one of compassion.

On November 26, 1504, in the fifty-fourth year of her life and the thirtieth year of her reign, Isabella of Castile died.

Despite her mistakes she was a great queen. Within her lifetime she and Ferdinand had raised their united kingdoms to world power. But to Isabella alone belongs the glory of the discoveries that would pour untold wealth into Spain.

"The world," wrote one of her contemporaries, "has lost one of its noblest ornaments. She was the mirror of every virtue, the shield of the innocent, the avenging sword to the wicked."

A mourning nation followed the queen's coffin to Granada. And there they buried her at the scene of her greatest triumph.

CATHERINE de' MEDICI

# 8

# CATHERINE DE' MEDICI:
## Madame Serpent

The birth of a child to the illustrious Medici family should have been a time of rejoicing. But Catherine was born into a world filled with sorrow. Her mother, Madeleine de la Tour d'Auvergne of the royal blood of France, died at her birth. Her father Lorenzo II, Duke de' Medici, survived his wife by only a few days. The little grandniece of Pope Leo X was an orphan.

Catherine was reared by a stern and deeply religious aunt, Clarissa Strozzi. The childhood years were divided between the courts of Rome and Florence. In times of strife—and there were many in those days—the little girl took refuge in the Murate Convent. There, young Catherine knew her happiest days. At the age of eleven she even expressed a desire to become a nun.

But the quiet convent life was not for this daughter of a powerful and wealthy family. The Medicis ranked among the noblest clans in Europe. Two popes, two queens of France, and numerous lesser luminaries came from their ranks. They were justly celebrated as advanced and enlightened humanitarians, scholars, and patrons of the arts. Thus it was not too difficult for her cousin Giulio, now Pope Clement VII, to arrange a brilliant marriage for the fourteen-year-old Catherine.

In 1533 she journeyed to France. There, resplendent in white satin gown and mantle of gem-encrusted gold, she became the bride of Henry, Duke of Orleans. Henry, a year older than his bride, was the second son of Francis I, King of France.

The French court was the gayest and most luxurious in all Europe. The still-young king had an eye for a pretty woman. His new daughter-in-law soon joined the band of beauties who rode and hunted and laughed with him. For Catherine was a splendid horsewoman. She was also extremely intelligent and well educated.

Her Medici heritage would in time have a widespread effect on the Renaissance of France. Her presence added a touch of unwonted elegance and refinement to the French court. Her personal library was said to contain 4,500 books and 776 ancient manuscripts. She was also a connoisseur and avid collector of art. Francis, at least, seems to have considered Catherine almost as welcome as her fabulous dowry.

Not so Prince Henry. He seemed completely immune to his wife's charms. At eighteen, Henry fell madly in love with the beautiful Diane de Poitiers. She was a widow and considerably older. But Henry never looked at another woman as long as he lived. That his loveless marriage was also a childless one did not appear important. Not at first.

In 1536, however, Henry's older brother died. Catherine now became Dauphiness of France. The lack of an heir began to loom large, and her future looked bleak. It cannot have comforted her to know that the audacious Diane was urging Henry to divorce his barren wife.

Such plans were thwarted only when a son was born to Catherine after ten years of marriage. Whatever triumph the new mother may have felt was soon dampened, however. The young prince was taken from her and given to Diane to rear. So were the nine other children that now followed in quick succession.

Diane also took charge of the tiny Queen of Scots when she came to France as the future bride of young Francis. Catherine probably did not resent this too much. She always despised the child. She overheard Mary refer to her scornfully as "the daughter of a merchant" and never forgave her. Besides, Mary Stuart was a niece of the powerful de Guise brothers. They were favored by the detested Diane, therefore hated by Catherine.

As long as Henry lived, his wife would remain a mere shadow. She was publicly humiliated by her husband and openly flouted by Diane. She was the laughingstock of the court and powerless in her own household. Small wonder, then, that the actions of her later years often smacked of insanity.

Not even the death of Francis I in 1547 could improve her sad lot. True, she was now officially queen of France. But it was Diane de Poitiers who ruled the king and, through him, the country.

Oddly enough, Catherine seemed to love her cruel and indifferent husband. She remained a faithful wife. Though she would eventually be accused of every possible crime, no breath of scandal ever touched her name. Loyally, she carried out whatever official duties Henry saw fit to assign her. Only once did she reap a reward.

In 1552, Paris itself was threatened with invasion. Catherine, acting as regent, promptly and courageously raised the men and money necessary to save the city. Henry graciously condescended to have a medal struck in her honor.

In 1559 Catherine was disturbed by a bad dream. She begged Henry not to enter the lists of the day's tournament. Henry laughed at her fears. But that day the entire court saw their king fall, mortally wounded by a lance thrust through the eye. Mary Stuart wrote her mother that Catherine was "plunged into such grief that I fear her misery will give her a bad illness."

The widowed queen, however, was not too grief-stricken to send the insufferable Diane packing almost before the king had breathed his last. In death, at least, Henry was hers alone.

Considering what she had suffered, Catherine was most forbearing with her rival. She demanded that Diane return the crown jewels she had worn for fifteen years, and she banished her from court forever. There were other rather petty persecutions, to be sure. But on the whole, Diane must have felt herself rather fortunate to escape so lightly.

The new king, Francis II, was weak and easily influenced by his mother. Catherine did not fail to take advantage of this to satisfy her hunger for power. When Francis died eighteen months later, the throne went to ten-year-old Charles. But it was Catherine de' Medici who ruled France as queen regent. In the next quarter century she was to make herself the most powerful and detested woman in French history.

Not only hated, but feared. People ceased to refer to her scornfully as "that Florentine shopkeeper." They now referred to her in whispers as "Madame Serpent."

Catherine was forty-one now. Her youthful grace and beauty had disappeared beneath ever-mounting layers of fat. But she was still vigorous and active, and those who opposed her soon felt the weight of her wrath. Indeed, if rumor is to be believed, not one person of consequence died a natural death during her reign. That is, not if that death could be construed as in any way favorable to the queen.

But ruling France proved no easy task. Religious quarrels had split the realm into two explosive factions. The hated de Guises led the Catholics; Admiral Coligny the Protestants. Catherine did her best to reconcile the two parties, but to no avail. Because she felt she could trust the admiral, her sympathies lay initially with the Huguenots, though she herself was a devout Catholic. But the Catholics were too strong. Persecutions of the Protestant sect increased.

It must be noted, in all fairness, that such persecutions were not all one-sided. The Protestants of Nimes, for instance, celebrated Michaelmas in 1567 by stuffing 154 of their Catholic fellow citizens down a well. And foreign mercenaries on both sides committed unspeakable atrocities at every opportunity.

When the inevitable civil war broke out, Catherine and Charles were seized by the de Guise faction. Partly because she was in their power, partly because she was furious with Coligny, Catherine cooperated. The admiral had turned the French cities of Havre and Calais over to the English. Catherine retaliated by keeping up a pretense of peace negotiations until Paris could be rescued by Spanish troops.

She then set about making peace. The assassination of Francis, Duke de Guise, made her task very difficult. Still she succeeded in bringing about the treaty of Amboise. It was a triumph for her policies. Truly, Catherine would "rather that the realm were at peace without God that at war with Him."

No sooner was internal peace established than Catherine rode out at the head of her troops to retake Havre. Fearlessly she exposed herself during the assault. Havre fell in what was almost a personal victory for the queen.

During all this, Catherine's relationship with her son was a strange and unnatural one. She hardly let the sensitive, high-strung lad out of her sight. She even insisted that he sleep in her bedroom at night. Charles could almost always be cajoled into doing what she wished. But, should he prove stubborn, she did not hesitate to play on his nerves or drive him into a hysterical frenzy. Nor did it matter that Charles was declared legally of age in 1563. His mother continued to rule exactly as before.

The religious wars flared anew. Again the violence was checked by Catherine's diplomacy. Concessions were made to the Huguenots. According to a contemporary writer, however, the queen mother "reserved to herself the pleasure of breaking her word." Especially, it would seem, to a Protestant.

Coligny now began to frequent the court. Charles liked him, and he soon gained what seemed to Catherine an undue amount of influence over the boy king. This she could not tolerate. Her plots began to thicken.

Hoping to bind the Protestants to the throne, Catherine proposed an alliance of marriage. Her daughter Marguerite was offered as a wife for Henry of Navarre, a Protestant champion. The match was arranged, though Henry's mother had long opposed it. "It is my wish, should you be married," she wrote her son, "that you and your wife should retire from this scene of corruption, which I find to be much worse than I had imagined." She was speaking of Catherine's court!

The wedding took place on August 18, 1572. Paris was crowded with Catholics and Huguenots who had flocked there for the four-day celebration. Sharp clashes were inevitable, and they were not long in coming. Coligny was wounded on the twenty-second as he was leaving the Louvre after an interview with the king. He was struck by a shot from an arquebus, allegedly fired by one of de Guise's men.

Little Charles was furious. He visited his wounded friend that same day. He also swore publicly to avenge him. The king's apparent sympathy encouraged the Huguenots to foolish audacities.

Wild rumors of a Huguenot plot began to fly. The king, it was whispered, was to be assassinated. Catherine made certain that every evil whisper was reported to Charles in all its gory detail. To her and her party this seemed a heaven-sent chance to rid themselves of the pestilential admiral. The unbalanced boy was terrified into a fit by their badgering.

"If you kill the admiral," he cried at last, "kill all the Huguenots in France, so that none shall be left to reproach me after it is done!" Then he ran from the room screaming, "Let them all be killed! Let them all be killed!"

And so there came about what has been described as "the greatest crime since the crucifixion"—the massacre, on St. Bartholemew's Day, of countless numbers of men, women, and children—the cruel and pitiful deaths of those whose only crime lay in holding the wrong religious beliefs.

Coligny was the first to die. His body was thrown from an upper window to be stomped and mutilated by de Guise and his followers. That was only the beginning. Huguenot nobles were hunted down and butchered within the palace itself. Only Henry of Navarre, the bridegroom, and the Prince de Conde were spared. Mobs raged throughout Paris. Every person they could lay their hands on who was even suspected of Protestant leanings was slain. The madness spread until such scenes of blood and carnage were repeated in every corner of France.

No amount of apology can ever absolve Catherine from responsibility for these terrible events. Even the king suffered bitter remorse. He also conceived a violent hatred for his mother. Catherine, it was said, was merely surprised that the remaining Huguenots continued to plague her.

Worse still, she had destroyed her precious balance of power. The de Guise faction grew ever more menacing.

Charles died pitifully in 1574—some say with the help of his mother. He rejoiced that he left no heir to his monstrous heritage. Catherine's third—and favorite—son now came to the throne as Henry III. He was the last, and the worst, of the Valois kings.

Though Henry was clearly insane, the aging queen mother could see no fault in her son. She could, and did, sacrifice her other children to this monster son's whims. She willingly surrendered her power to him. She was content to do his bidding. She traveled the land unceasingly for him. On the way she plotted, bribed, cajoled and probably murdered to keep the ungrateful Henry on the throne.

In 1587 the "War of the Three Henrys" broke out. It was simply a struggle for personal power among Henry III, Henry, Duke de Guise, and Henry of Navarre. Almost from the first, things went badly for the royal cause. The duke took Paris and held the king prisoner.

Henry managed to escape and took refuge at Blois. There he submitted to demands that he convoke the States General. De Guise was now so confident of final victory that he grew careless. He made the mistake of going alone to an early morning council meeting in answer to a summons from the king. There he met death at the hands of Henry's bodyguard.

Catherine lay ill in another part of the castle. She was still plotting—still hoping to play her old game of balancing one faction against another. When Henry burst in upon her with the news of the duke's assassination, she was horror-stricken.

"May God annihilate me," she cried, "if I ever dreamed this crime or counseled it!"

For Catherine knew all too well that Henry had made a fatal blunder.

"The figure of Catherine de' Medici," wrote Balzac, "stands out as that of a great king. Indeed, as long as she lived the House of Valois sat on the throne." Whether or not Catherine could have found a remedy for her son's latest insanity is debatable. She did not long survive her old enemy.

She did not live to see the final downfall of the house she had kept on the throne. She did not witness King Henry's own assassination seven months later. She was not subjected to the spectacle of Henry of Navarre, first of the Bourbon kings, sitting on the Valois throne.

Catherine died January 5, 1589.

Her end was as bleak and comfortless as her beginning.

"A few servants wept for her," said one chronicler, "and so did the king—a little."

MARY TUDOR

# 9

# MARY TUDOR:
## Queen of Tragedy

The seventeen-year-old girl faced the members of the king's privy council without flinching. Perhaps, under that calm gaze, a few had the grace to drop their eyes guiltily. It was a shabby thing they were doing.

But after all, the girl was no fool. Surely she had been expecting something of the sort.

"By the king's high commandment," the Lady Mary must lay aside the title and dignity of princess. She must forbid her servants to address her as such. Furthermore, she must withdraw immediately from court. Since the duly appointed courts of law had declared the marriage of her parents null and void, she could hardly expect to be treated with royal honors.

Mary heard them out. But her reply showed more courage than humility.

"Unless I am informed by a letter from the king's own hand that His Grace wishes to diminish my name, state, and dignity, I shall never believe it. Then, my lords, I will obey His Grace, as my duty is."

Though she knew appeal was hopeless, she felt she must defend herself and her mother. "But I do protest before you that my conscience will in no way suffer me to believe myself other than a princess, or a king's daughter born in lawful matrimony. Nor do I say this out of any ambition or proud mind, as God is my judge. If I should do otherwise it should dishonor the king my father and the queen my mother and confess my own birth illegitimate, which God forbid I should do. The pope himself has not so declared it, and to his judgment I submit myself."

Thus were the battle lines drawn between Mary Tudor and her cruel and ruthless father, Henry VIII. But it had not always been so.

Born at Greenwich, February 18, 1516, Mary was the only surviving child of Henry and his first wife, Catherine of Aragon. She was a pretty child, healthy, happy, and precocious. She was given the elaborate education considered suitable for a Renaissance princess. She early mastered several languages, including French, Italian, and Spanish. Latin was learned as a matter of course since it was the language of diplomacy. She showed a decided talent for music and practiced for hours upon the virginals, a forerunner of the piano.

Mary was also an avid reader. However, she was not

allowed to read those idle romances so "corrupting to the morals of young girls." Her books were heavy and uplifting religious tomes. Religion, indeed, played an important part in the life of the young princess; her devout Spanish Catholic mother saw to that.

The usual glittering matches with the crowned heads of Europe were proposed for this sprig of English royalty. She was betrothed at age of three to the Dauphin of France. This match was broken off for a better offer from the Emperor Charles V when she was six.

Life at the pleasure-loving Henry's court was a gay round of pageants, tournaments, and balls. The teen-age princess was allowed to join in the festivities and was very popular. The king was proud of her. He led her through the rollicking dances. Once he removed her jeweled hairnet with his own hands so that all might see her "profusion of fair hair, as beautiful as ever seen on a human head."

Henry, however, made no secret of his passionate desire for a son. The lack of a male heir was the excuse he used when he began to hint that all was not well in his marriage. The real reason, of course, was that Henry had fallen madly in love with Anne Boleyn.

When the divorce came, Mary was at an age to feel the humiliations most keenly. Her plunge from pampered princess and heiress presumptive was a shattering one. Not even the honorable retreat of marriage was open to her. Her engagement to Charles was broken and no suitable match was available. Then too, Henry had been forced to break with the pope and declare himself head of the English Church in order to obtain the divorce. The devout Mary could not abandon her faith so easily.

Catherine feared for her daughter's very life if she

provoked Henry too far. Though cruelly separated from her child, she wrote often. She cautioned Mary to "speak few words and meddle in nothing." Mary stubbornly refused to deny either her mother's rights as queen or the Roman Catholic beliefs.

The birth of Princess Elizabeth brought matters to a head. To assure the rights of this daughter of Anne Boleyn, an Act of Succession was passed. The new princess was made heir to the throne while Mary was declared legally fatherless. To a demand that she pay homage to her rival, Mary replied, "Sister I will call the babe, but nothing more."

Mary's princely establishment at Beaulieu was dissolved. Her servants and friends were sent away and Mary was ordered to remove herself to the "nursery palace" of Hunsdon. Here, she was reduced to the status of a poor relation in the sumptuous household of Elizabeth. Several persons were sent to the Tower for daring to address the poor girl as "Princess."

Oddly enough, the disgraced princess never seemed to hold her baby sister responsible for her woes. She even learned to love the child who displaced her. It was, in fact, Mary who supervised the child's early education.

Mary was separated from her mother by royal command. Not even when Catherine lay dying in 1534 was she allowed the comfort of a farewell visit. Still, while Catherine lived, Mary had not been completely alone in the world. Now she was alone. And hers was a hostile world shadowed with the ever-present threat of the Tower should she provoke Henry too far.

Perhaps she found some comfort in the fact that the hated Anne Boleyn outlived Catherine by a scant five months. The night before her execution for high treason, Anne sent a message to the girl she had helped to wrong. Lady Kingston was instructed to "fall down before Mary and beg her forgiveness."

Henry married again before his second wife was cold in her grave. The reign of Jane Seymour—whom Mary could honestly regard as a legitimate wife—made life a little easier for the girl. For two years Henry had deprived her of all but the barest necessities. She had been humiliated, bullied, and threatened because she would neither admit the legality of the divorce nor acknowledge Henry as head of the Church. She had seen monasteries burned and abbots and monks hanged from their own gates. She had seen nuns driven into the streets, shrines sacked, and churches pulled down. Her friends and advisers were gone, many of them condemned to death because of their faith.

Devout and courageous as she was, Mary could no longer hold out. She signed the required statements.

Henry was so delighted that he allowed her a household of her own once more. She was even allowed a certain amount of freedom, especially after his only son, Edward, was born. Mary and Elizabeth were allowed to take part in the boy's christening. And it was Mary who managed the court during the period of mourning for Queen Jane, who died two weeks later.

Unfortunately, Mary soon became the focal point of Catholic discontent. She retired once more to Elizabeth's household at Hertford. Three years were to pass before she was welcomed at court again. She was allowed to ride in the wedding procession of Henry's fourth wife, the quickly divorced Anne of Cleves.

Henry's favor was soon withdrawn. A Catholic uprising

sent many of Mary's friends to the scaffold and placed her own head in danger. Her household was dissolved yet again, and she was in dire poverty for some time.

Meanwhile, Henry continued his bewildering matrimonial merry-go-round. He married Catherine Howard, but she soon followed her cousin, Anne Boleyn, to a traitor's death. His last wife, Catherine Parr, befriended Mary. It was undoubtedly her influence which restored the two scorned princesses to their father's favor. She also made sure that their rights of succession were insured in his will.

A marriage for Mary was negotiated in 1540. Duke Philip of Bavaria broke off negotiations because of Henry's outrageous behavior. Another proposed match, this time with a French prince, fell through because Mary's dowry was too small.

Mary was only in her mid-twenties, but hardship and disappointment had made her bitter and neurotic. She withdrew more and more and devoted herself to her prayers, her music, and her embroidery. Her pious attitude and reproachful eyes often tried Henry's patience sorely. Still, thanks to Catherine, she remained more or less in favor until her father's death.

Henry even offered a sort of apology before he died. He told her that he knew she had suffered, that "fortune had been adverse" to her. Still, she must blame it on the will of God or "your own ill-luck." He then exacted a promise from her that she should "remain as a kind and loving mother to your brother, whom I shall leave as a helpless little child."

Mary promised willingly, for she was greatly attached to the frail Edward. After Henry's death in 1547, she would have kept the promise had she been allowed to do so. As it was, the fleeting years of Edward's reign were sad ones for her. The boy king was completely controlled by his Protestant regents.

The persecution of the Catholic princess was resumed. She was banished from court. Her religious views were attacked, and only the threat of an invasion by Charles V insured her right to worship as she pleased. Worry and privation brought on an illness from which she would never completely recover.

Edward died in 1553. In his will both Mary and Elizabeth were cut out of the succession in favor of Lady Jane Grey. Not content with this, the Protestant lords sent a message to Mary in the name of her dead brother. They hoped to lure her into a trap and destroy her before anyone knew the king was dead.

Mary was warned in time. Little Lady Jane was hurriedly placed on the throne by her Protestant supporters, but Mary soon learned that the people supported Henry's daughter. In this crisis she acted swiftly and courageously.

Her campaign began with neither money, men, nor advisers. Yet within eight days she had rallied enough support to drive the usurper from the throne and send her enemies scattering. Her triumphal entry into London was greeted with wild enthusiasm by the people. It seemed only fitting that this princess who had suffered so much should take her rightful place at last.

In May, Mary Tudor became England's first crowned queen in a splendid coronation ceremony.

The reign began well. The new queen showed herself merciful in refusing to execute Lady Jane Grey. She declared that she knew the child to be only an innocent tool. She showed herself just by putting an end to bribery in her courts. She showed herself honest by accepting the responsibility of her father's debts, which she might legally have repudiated.

At first, Mary even showed herself tolerant in religious matters. The parish churches were restored, of course, but she made no move to suppress the Protestants. She *did* refuse to accept the title of head of the English Church, but with a note of unexpected humor.

"Women, I have read in the Scriptures, are forbidden to speak in the church. Is it, then fitting that your Church should have a dumb head?"

Naturally, her first Parliament removed the stigma of illegitimacy from her birth—and put it squarely on Elizabeth's. This was a mistake. Elizabeth was already becoming the fair-haired hope of the Protestant cause. Mary could hardly help being aware of this. Still, she took no steps against her sister beyond forcing her to attend mass.

That same Parliament discussed the question of the queen's marriage—to no purpose, really, for Mary had already fallen in love with a portrait of Philip II of Spain and would have no other. Her determination caused a furor. The English hated and distrusted everything Spanish. Mary coolly informed Parliament that her choice of a husband was none of its business and forthwith dissolved it.

This proved to be a near-fatal blunder. Plots to depose Mary sprang up on every hand. Rebellion flared in the West Country, and Thomas Wyatt led an uprising in Kent. His avowed purpose was to depose Mary and place Elizabeth on the throne.

Once again Mary showed herself cool and courageous in an emergency. Wyatt's men were already swarming into London. The queen was in great danger of being captured if she remained at Whitehall. Her advisers urged her to flee to the safety of the Tower.

"If I do that, I lose my crown," was her reply.

Instead, she went in person among the people of London. She appealed for their loyal support, promising that she would contract no marriage to the detriment of the realm. When they declared themselves overwhelmingly for her, the rebellion was doomed.

Now the persecutions began. Wyatt and Lady Jane Grey led a long line of victims to scaffold and gibbet. Elizabeth walked in fear of her life. But Mary still retained her old affection, and her sister escaped with only a bad fright.

Meanwhile, Mary pursued her purpose of marrying Philip. Judicious bribes won the support of many of her nobles. And the people's opposition was somewhat lessened by the sight of twenty cartloads of Spanish gold. These were paraded ostentatiously through the streets and deposited in the Tower "for the queen's use." At least this foreign prince had not come to rob them.

Perhaps Mary knew the only moments of true happiness in her adult life as she walked to the altar to be wed. She was now thirty-six, and her youthful good looks had long since faded. No amount of diamond-embroidered satin and brocade could make her young again. No black velvet mantle and red satin slippers could make her beautiful. Only the joyous surge of love and the honest belief that her love was returned could do that. The young and handsome Philip had played his part well.

Her happiness was short-lived. Quarrels between Philip's followers and the English broke out. In the end, not even another £150,000 in gold bullion could buy English toleration. They even made fun of Philip's small stature in the nursery rhyme that goes, "I had a little husband, no bigger than my thumb."

Worst of all, Parliament staunchly refused to allow Philip any share in the government. The only concession Philip could wangle was a grudging consent to reconciliation with the Church of Rome.

This was Mary's final triumph.

Philip, disgusted with her and her barbarous country, ceased to woo her. Mary turned to religion for consolation. This latest disillusionment seems to have been too much for her mind. She conceived the notion that God was punishing her for her toleration of the Protestant heresies.

It is to Philip's credit that he advised against the course his wife was about to take. But he left England after a little more than a year. Mary embarked on the persecutions which were to earn her the infamous title of "Bloody Mary."

She was indeed in a pitiable state. The child she had confidently expected turned out to be a false pregnancy, Philip had walked out on her, and there were conspirators wherever she looked. She increased the frenzy of the Smithfield burnings. But not even the death of the man who had engineered her mother's disgrace could console her. She grieved until she received word that Philip was returning.

It was not the return of a loving husband, however. Philip merely wanted her support in his war against

France. He got his ten thousand men by threatening to go and never return.

But Mary had made her sacrifice and angered her people for nothing. The war went badly. The only result was the loss of the English-held port of Calais. It was the last of England's once-mighty continental possessions. Its fall in 1558 was the crowning failure of a long line of failures for Mary Tudor.

Perhaps the three months of Philip's company so dearly bought might have been worth it except for one thing. Mary soon learned that her loving husband had spent his spare time plotting to put Elizabeth on her throne. In despair, the betrayed queen took a knife and slashed Philip's portrait to ribbons.

Then, declaring that if her breast were opened "Calais" would be found written on her heart, she sank into her last illness.

The end approached for the forty-year-old queen, alone and friendless in the echoing palace of St. James.

Philip did not come to her.

No one came. All the court, including her husband's authorized representative, were crowding the road to Hatfield.

There, the rising star, Elizabeth, awaited them.

ELIZABETH I

# 10

# ELIZABETH I:
# Bride of England

Elizabeth regarded with a cold eye the courtiers who thronged toward her country retreat. She knew that they had left Queen Mary to die alone. Even in this moment of triumph, that knowledge disgusted and frightened her.

It also taught her a valuable lesson. To the nobility, a monarch commanded respect only so long as he had power. Only the common people ever gave their hearts to a sovereign. Only they had time to mourn the one they loved. These nobles were like rats deserting a sinking ship.

Elizabeth was not foolish enough to believe that those who now knelt at her feet did so out of any affection for her. Only a short while before she had been shunned by all but a few of them. Even now, should Mary by some miracle recover, they would run away as quickly as they had come.

But the little people—ah, that was different! Whenever she rode through the streets of London she could *feel* their love reach out to her. Between her and them there was a good bond like a living thing. Even when she was in the deepest disgrace they had cheered for her.

These, then, were her people. Not the peers of the realm, but the shopkeepers, the sailors, the inkeepers, the weavers and bakers and masons. These were England, and she would be England's queen!

Elizabeth never forgot the lesson. She seldom forgot anything, for that matter. The rough schooling of a childhood fraught with peril—a girlhood hemmed in by treachery was not wasted. Almost from the day of her birth in 1533, Elizabeth had been subject to the whims of her royal sire. And Henry VIII was capable of monstrous tyrannies. Consider the testimony of the French ambassador.

"I have to do," he wrote, "with the most dangerous and cruel man in the world." If an experienced diplomat was so terrified that he begged to be recalled, what chance had a three-year-old child?

At times, Elizabeth was a coddled and cherished favorite. At other times she was banished to the loneliness of some isolated manor house and treated with cold contempt by king and court. Such sudden changes must have been bewildering to a small child.

"How haps it, Governor?" she asked. "Yesterday My Lady Princess and today but My Lady Elizabeth?"

She was shamefully neglected after her mother's disgrace. Her governess was forced to beg for money to clothe a princess who had "neither gown, nor kirtle, nor petticoat, nor no manner of linen. . . ." Fortunately, her education was not equally neglected. She had early shown signs of an unusual intellect.

By nine she was studying history, geography, mathematics, architecture, and astronomy. She spoke and wrote fluently in French, Italian, Spanish, Flemish, Greek, and Latin. Later she added Welsh to her formidable array of languages. She learned it from a servant.

More important than her formal schooling perhaps, she acquired a thorough grounding in the intricate science of intrigue and the gentle art of double-dealing. These were to stand her in good stead throughout her life.

Elizabeth was fourteen when Henry died and, for the moment, in his good graces. Edward's tragically short reign did little to improve her lot. She was caught in the struggle of the Seymour brothers for control of the young king. A girlish crush on the dashing Thomas Seymour brought her perilously close to being indicted for treason. Thomas lost the struggle—and his head as well.

Nor did her sister's accession help Elizabeth. The reign of Catholic Mary of necessity placed the life of Protestant Elizabeth in jeopardy. For a time it looked as if the unfortunate princess was doomed to follow her mother to the block.

The terrified Elizabeth was actually sent to the Tower once, and for good reason. Whether or not she was aware of the plot, the ill-starred Wyatt's Rebellion had been raised in her name. Elizabeth, of course, denied everything. She balked at entering the menacing Traitor's Gate.

"Here lands as true a subject," she cried, "as ever landed at these stairs."

This may have been true. But no matter how innocent her intentions, her very existence and her popularity made her a constant threat to Mary. It is to that queen's credit that she did not rid herself of such a rival when she had the chance.

Fortunately, the dying Wyatt cleared Elizabeth's name. After a harrowing two months, she was removed from the Tower and sent to the less rigorous confinement of Woodstock. It cannot have helped Elizabeth's cause with Mary that she was cheered enthusiastically all the way. It was at Woodstock that she cut the famous lines into a window-pane with her diamond.

> "Much suspected, by me,
> Nothing proved can be,
> Quoth Elizabeth, prisoner."

It was perhaps the very uncertainties of those early days that forged the strong and self-reliant character of this remarkable woman. Certainly it was no winsome, dainty miss who entered London to the wild acclamation of the crowds that lined her way. In the dazzling young queen with her tawny hair, startlingly white skin, and golden-brown eyes they recognized a true daughter of the Tudors.

And so began the romance between Elizabeth Tudor and her realm which was to last for nearly half a century.

Dressed in crimson velvet and ermine, she was crowned queen on January 15, 1559. The coronation vows she took then were never lightly set aside. England was her love, her life. Never would she set foot outside its borders, not even to visit neighboring Scotland or Wales.

"Have a care over my people," she admonished her judges. "They are *my* people—see unto them, for they are my charge."

And when the usual question of marriage came up, Elizabeth held up the hand which bore the heavy coronation ring.

"I am already bound to a bridegroom which is the Kingdom of England!"

Actually, Elizabeth had never swerved from her childhood determination not to marry. Her adolescent love affair with Thomas Seymour was probably genuine enough, at least on her part. But never again would Elizabeth Tudor risk her head—or her crown—at the dictates of her heart. Nor would she submit to domination by any man. Even her trusted ministers and long-time favorites often felt the weight of her wrath if they overstepped the mark.

"God's death, my lord!" she would roar. "I will have but one mistress here and no master!"

One thing that endeared Elizabeth to her people was an economy which amounted almost to stinginess. She spent every farthing of public money as grudgingly as if it had been her own. The last six months of Mary's reign had cost £267,000. Elizabeth spent only £108,000 in the first six months of hers. And never did her budget exceed £500,000.

Not that Elizabeth had no love for luxuries. She did, but she indulged her taste for extravagant clothes and jewels and furniture without parting with her own gold pieces. She encouraged—almost demanded—ruinously expensive presents from her wealthier subjects.

It took her fifteen years to do it, but she paid back every penny of the enormous debt owed to the City of London by Henry and Edward.

There was about her a lusty quality which appealed to the lusty people who made up the rank and file of her realm. Lytton Strachey tells us that "she swore, she spat, she struck with her fist when she was angry, she roared with laughter when she was amused." And she surrounded herself with the most able administrators she could find, never caring if they were nobles or commoners.

Finally, like her father before her, Elizabeth had a keen interest in the navy, so dear to English hearts. To protect her merchant fleet, she commissioned as many new warships as she could afford. Many a commercial venture, including the piratical forays of her "Sea Dogs," was backed by Elizabeth's private purse. Nor can we scoff at such investments. She realized a tidy profit of 1400 per cent on Drake's famous voyage in the *Golden Hind!*

Not even the burning question of religion marred the first honeymoon years of the reign. Elizabeth was prepared to be tolerant, though many of her advisers were not.

"There is but one Jesus Christ," she said, "and one faith. The rest is a dispute about trifles."

Henry's doctrines, naturally, were reinstated. Only through them could she lay claim to the throne. But there the matter rested. In the first ten years of the reign not a single death sentence was passed.

Only the question of the succession really haunted her. Though she had no intention of marrying, it delighted her to play the game of courtship. Negotiations would be dragged out interminably as long as there was a political advantage to be gained. But in the end every proposal was rejected. England undoubtedly needed an heir, but that was the one thing Elizabeth was not prepared to give.

Mary of Scotland had long been eying the throne to which she had a valid claim. Her marriage to the equally eligible and aspiring Lord Darnley infuriated Elizabeth. Still, she could not bring herself to name an heir. She feared that to do so would be to invite her own assassination. News of the birth of Mary's son struck fear in Elizabeth's heart.

"The Queen of Scots is lighter of a fair son," she moaned, "and I am but barren stock!"

Because of this she kept a close eye on the developing tragedy across the border. She declared Mary's reported behavior so idiotic that it could not be true. Nevertheless, she felt enough concern for her cousin to threaten an invasion if Mary were harmed. It was only when Mary fled to England that she presented Elizabeth with almost insurmountable problems.

It was impossible to allow the dethroned queen to roam at will. She would be the rallying point for every Catholic plot. It was equally impossible to be rid of her without bringing down the hornet's nest of a Spanish invasion on Elizabeth's ill-defended realm. Aside from an unsuccessful attempt to return Mary to Scotland, there was nothing to do but keep her prisoner.

Even so, Elizabeth was in constant fear of assassination. At least four major plots were uncovered. To kill Elizabeth and place Mary on the throne had become for many, the focus of their lives.

That Elizabeth escaped was almost a miracle. Once she

recognized among the crowds as she walked in a park, one of "six gentlemen" who had sworn to destroy her.

"Am I not well guarded today," she chided, "with no man near me who wears a sword?"

And one plot failed only because the would-be assassin hesitated to strike. She reminded him too much, he said, of Henry VIII!

In the end, the Scots queen overreached herself and sentence of death was passed against her. Elizabeth agonized long before signing the death warrant. She was heard to mutter, "Strike or be stricken, strike or be stricken," in pitiful repetition. Knowing full well that the execution would provoke the war she dreaded above all else, she resorted to trickery. She signed the fatal document but pretended it was put into effect without her knowledge or consent.

This pretense was childishly transparent. It deserved to fail, and it did. The Spanish Armada was soon on its way.

Nowhere is the close relationship of Elizabeth and her people more dramatic than in this time of crisis. She could not summon her army and navy. She had none worthy of the name. Instead, she appealed directly to the people. The response was overwhelming.

"We will not bandy words," she told the lord mayor of London. "The Spanish fleet is almost upon us. We need fifteen ships and five thousand men without delay. Can London furnish them?"

The lord mayor smiled as he bowed before her.

"Had your Majesty not sent for me when you did, I should have been obliged to seek an audience," he replied. "The City of London, knowing the need, has already mustered its forces. We are prepared to offer, not fifteen ships and five thousand men, but thirty ships and ten thousand men!"

Mounted on a white charger and resplendent in a breastplate of polished steel, Elizabeth reviewed her troops at Tilbury.

"I know I have the body of a weak and feeble woman," she told them. "But I have the heart and stomach of a king, and a king of England too!"

The men greeted her speech with a mighty roar of approval. Every heart was touched, and every man swore he would willingly die for so gallant a queen. They would have done it too, except that it turned out to be unnecessary. The "Invincible Armada" was driven off after a four-day running battle at sea. The work of destruction so well begun by the fast-sailing little English ships was completed by terrible gales. The Spanish fleet was shattered without so much as touching English shores.

England was now mistress of the seas. And Elizabeth was still mistress of England.

The English people could now develop their industries in peace. They could plant their colonies and establish their trade routes. They could practice their religion without fear of outside interference. Truly, they had entered fully into the golden age which would forever after be known as Elizabethan.

The realm that had been torn by religious quarrels and civil strife was welded into a strong national unit. In an atmosphere of peace and plenty, art could flourish. Men like Shakespeare and Marlowe and Spenser could write their masterpieces. Bawdy comedies, stirring dramas, and exquisitely lyrical poetry flowed from their pens.

Music, too, was an essential part of the Elizabethan

scene. Every member of the nobility played one or more musical instruments. And even the peasants excelled in singing the lovely compositions of the age. Dancing was all the rage. Elizabeth prided herself on her ability to perform the lively and complex dances of the day. The poorer classes celebrated their old pagan festivals with dances around the maypole or the bonfires of midsummer. The Yule season especially was a time of merriment and feasting for all classes.

But the queen who made it all possible was growing old. The men who had served her so faithfully were dying. Elizabeth loathed the idea of aging. She resorted to bizarre costumes literally crusted with gems, to ridiculous ruffs and hideous red wigs and clownlike makeup to hide the ravages of time. When all else failed, we are told, she refused to allow mirrors in her palaces.

It was probably for the same reason that she surrounded herself with a new generation of brash young favorites. They may or may not have been genuinely fond of their still-vain monarch. But they were willing to flatter her unmercifully and give her the illusion that she was still desirable. It is certain that they truly loved the wealth and power her favor gave them.

"When will you cease to be a beggar, Raleigh?" she asked the founder of Virginia.

"When your majesty ceases to be a benefactor," came the young man's bold reply.

Another, even more arrogant favorite, was Robert Devereux, Earl of Essex. He remained in her good graces for fifteen years. But finally he went too far. Furious at what she considered his disobedience to her orders, Elizabeth

( 124 )

sent him to the Tower for nearly a year. Even when he was released, she refused to see him.

Essex deeply resented such treatment. Probably in the belief that the queen was still too enamored of him to punish him as he deserved, he allowed himself to become involved in a treasonous plot. In so doing, he misjudged Elizabeth's temperament completely.

His execution as a traitor saddened the queen. But she said only, "I had put up with but too much disrespect to my person, but I warned him that he should not touch my scepter."

Essex was beheaded in 1601. That same year Elizabeth, her frail body weighted down by her robes of state, stumbled on the steps of her throne at the opening of Parliament. Soon afterward the coronation ring she had worn for forty-five years had to be cut from her badly swollen finger.

Elizabeth considered both events as bad omens.

She was nearing seventy now and growing steadily weaker. Only her indomitable will kept her going. She refused to take to her bed for fear her people would think she was dying.

In January of 1603, the queen contracted a bad cold which would not be shaken off. By the end of February it was clear that she was dying. Still, she had enough spirit left to rebuke the physician who told her she must rest.

"Little man," she snapped, "the word 'must' is not to be used to princes!"

Word that the end was near for their beloved queen spread rapidly throughout London. "A strange silence descended on the whole city." Only when that end was at hand did she indicate by signs that Mary Stuart's son, James VI of Scotland, was to be her heir.

On March 25, Elizabeth, last and greatest of the Tudor monarchs, closed her eyes in death.

The "bride" was gone and the "bridegroom" mourned her going deeply and sincerely. England under Elizabeth was not heaven on earth. There were many abuses, and life was extremely harsh for the poor and oppressed. Still, most Elizabethans felt that Merrie England would do well enough until heaven came along.

Of her people, Elizabeth had said, "I do not so much rejoice that God hath made me Queen as to be Queen over so thankful a people."

And the response of her people may be summed up in the simple words of one of them:

"We loved her because she said she did love us."

MARY STUART

# I I

# MARY STUART:
## Queen of Hearts

James V lay ill in body and sick at heart. He had lost interest in everything since the senseless defeat of his armies at Solway Moss. Not even the exciting news seemed to arouse him. His queen, Mary de Guise, had given him an heir. The child had been born at Linlithgow Palace on December 8, 1542.

The king roused himself only enough to demand, "A manchild or a woman?"

The answer was slow in coming. "A fair daughter, Sire."

"The devil go with it!" cried James. "Adieu, farewell. It came with a lass and it will pass with a lass!"

And he turned his face to the wall and spoke no more.

Six days later James V was dead. The "lass" was Queen of Scotland.

Despite her father's gloomy predictions, the fates seemed determined to heap favors on the red-gold head of little Mary Stuart. Marriage proposals were showered on the infant before she cut her first tooth. Henry VIII of England demanded her hand for his heir, Prince Edward. The Scots Parliament refused.

Enraged, Henry sent an army into Scotland. His orders: "Burn Edinburgh town, sack Holyrood House, putting man, woman and child to fire and sword without exception. . . ." The Scots ruefully called this "The Rough Wooing." It was the first, but not the last time, the matrimonial plans of the Queen of Scots would lead to bloodshed.

Henry's raid only served to drive the stubborn Scots into the arms of the French. Their tiny queen was formally bethrothed to the eldest son of Henry II. At five, Mary was whisked across the Channel to the glittering French court. There she would receive the education befitting a future queen of France.

Mary was a remarkably charming and intelligent child. She soon captured the hearts of all who came in contact with her. The one exception was her future mother-in-law, Catherine de' Medici, who always detested her. But it was the French king himself who helped Mary make an even more dangerous enemy.

When Mary Tudor died, Henry immediately proclaimed his little ward as Queen of England. English arms were emblazoned on her carriages. In so doing he and Mary completely ignored Elizabeth's claim to—and possession of—that throne. Elizabeth never forgave her cousin the insult.

Mary grew and flourished at the French court. She was carefully educated for the thrones she would one day occupy. At the age of twelve she was given a household of her own and declared old enough to manage her own affairs. Her first act was to make her mother regent of Scotland.

Mary de Guise struggled valiantly to keep her daughter's realm intact. Hers also was the thankless task of collecting the £60,000 to finance the royal wedding. It is just as well that the surly Scots never knew that their young queen virtually gave Scotland to France in her marriage contract.

The wedding took place under a blue silk pavilion in the square before Notre Dame Cathedral. Everyone agreed that the bride was breathtakingly beautiful in her blue velvet robes and golden coronet. She was barely fifteen years old. Her frail little bridegroom was a year younger. Still, in spite of their extreme youth, the marriage was a happy one.

Within a year Henry II was killed in a tournament. Mary of Scotland was now Queen of France, but her glory was short-lived. Eighteen months later, she was a widow. The untimely death of her boy husband followed closely upon that of her mother. The not yet eighteen-year-old queen was alone and friendless. Catherine de' Medici was now regent for her second son. She made it quite clear to Mary that there was no room in France for *two* dowager queens.

In August, 1561, a saddened Mary Stuart returned to the land of her birth.

It was not a happy homecoming. The queen, fearing

capture by the English, had set sail unexpectedly early. Consequently, nothing was ready to receive her. She landed in a smothering fog, and spent the first night in her realm at the humble house of a merchant at Leith.

Nor were things much better later. The stiff-necked lairds of Scotland had never bowed willingly before the throne. Now many of them had abandoned Catholicism for Calvinism under the fanatic leadership of John Knox. And Mary was not only a woman but a devout Catholic to boot.

Compared to the warmth and luxury of France, Scotland was a cold barbaric land. The contrast must have appalled the delicately reared queen. Nevertheless, she made the best of her poor, rough land. She set herself to charm her subjects, and she succeeded with many.

Dour old John Knox was much discomfited to see his recent converts flocking to kiss the hand of a Catholic monarch. One, Mary's half-brother, James Stuart, even stood guard with drawn sword before the little chapel at Holyrood. This was necessary in order that his sister might hear mass undisturbed. But Mary's charm foundered on the rock of the reformer's disapproval. It was the question of religion which denied her the unqualified acclaim of her people.

Nevertheless, the young queen assumed the reins of her government with a sure hand. For a while she ruled both wisely and well. Her tact and diplomacy did much to soothe the turbulent quarrels of her nobles. She also brought many refinements to the grim Scottish court. The halls of Holyrood Palace soon resounded to music and laughter. Mary introduced such French pastimes as dancing and pageants and masked balls. John Knox could only shake his head darkly at such sinful goings-on and mutter darkly of retribution.

Notable—for more reasons than one—was the wedding celebration at Crichton. John Stuart, another of Mary's half-brothers, was marrying the sister of James Hepburn, Earl of Bothwell. Eighteen hundred wild deer are said to have been roasted for the wedding banquet, which was graced by the queen's own presence.

Mary had reason to be grateful to Bothwell. He had served her mother well during the dark days of the regency. Now in his late twenties, Bothwell had lived a full and adventurous life. History has condemned him as an ignorant and savage brawler—a borderer singularly lacking in breeding and morals. Some of the charges may be justified, but not all. James Hepburn had a Paris education and probably was as polished a courtier as any at Mary's disposal. Nevertheless, he fell under her displeasure soon after her return. He was first imprisoned, then exiled.

The question of a second marriage loomed large on Mary's political horizon. Both the Swedish and Danish kings were suing for her hand. Mary herself preferred a Spanish alliance. Her subjects had other ideas. Each Scottish faction had its own candidate for the queen's consort. And each hoped to gain control of the realm through him. Even Elizabeth of England got into the act. She sweetly offered one of her own cast-off suitors, and was considerably miffed when the furious Mary spurned him.

Mary settled the matter by falling in love. She wilfully married her cousin, Lord Darnley. Since he was English with a claim to the English throne almost as good as

Mary's own, the marriage enraged Elizabeth. In fact, it pleased no one except the bride and groom. And Mary soon had reason to regret her hasty choice.

Darnley proved to be no more than a handsome, selfish fop—a weakling without a shred of honesty or integrity. Piqued at her refusal to grant him full powers as king, he turned against her. He openly accused his wife of gross misconduct with her Italian secretary, Rizzio. He then joined a group of discontented nobles in a plot to kidnap the queen. One of their most vicious acts was the murder of the lame Rizzio in Mary's presence.

Mary cunningly hid her loathing for Darnley long enough to persuade the posturing fool to free her. After that she suffered his presence for only one reason. Their son, born two months after the murder, must first be christened and acknowledged rightful heir to the throne. Once this was accomplished, the queen no longer troubled to hide her contempt. Darnley was all but banished.

It is not certain when Mary actually fell in love with the dashing Earl of Bothwell. He had returned from exile, and now we find him constantly in her service and often at her side. He accepted her love. There is much room to doubt, however, that he actually returned it. In wooing her he was probably inspired by no more tender a sentiment than driving ambition. At any rate, Darnley had now become a stumbling block in the path of true love.

The plan to murder the unwanted husband was probably Bothwell's. Violence was part and parcel of his character. Even the doting Mary called him a "glorious, rash and hazardous man." Still, the queen was by no means as innocent as some of her defenders would have us believe. She was implicated at least to the extent of luring the unsuspecting victim into the trap.

It was Mary who made peaceful overtures to her estranged husband. It was she who brought an invalid recuperating from smallpox from Glasgow in midwinter. It was she who arranged to lodge him in the house at Kirk o' Field just outside Edinburgh. It was she who spent two nights there and was "fortunately" called away on the third.

Mary was not there when the explosions rocked the city at two in the morning.

Excited townspeople found only gaping cellars where the king's house had stood. Darnley, of course, was dead. But not, it was whispered, from the effects of the blast. His body was found in the garden apparently untouched by concussion or fire, but dead just the same—strangled, in fact.

For the first time, Mary heard the voices of her people raised against her instead of her religion. To hush some of the gossip, Bothwell was tried for the murder. His acquittal was worse than useless. The world knew it was because none had the courage to testify against him. Many, indeed, could not. He held positive proof that they were as guilty as he.

Even so, Mary might have kept her throne. She threw away her last chance by rashly marrying the accused murderer.

The ill-timed wedding roused her nobles to fury. They may have plotted Darnley's murder with Bothwell, but they would not stand by and see him make himself their king. The newlyweds were forced to flee from Edinburgh to seek out supporters.

After some hairbreadth escapes, Mary found her army. Her forces were drawn up for battle at Carberry Hill in June of 1567. But the enemy cleverly delayed attack until the "loyal" soldiers began to melt away. Mary, seeing it was hopeless, agreed to surrender without a fight, on one condition. She demanded that Bothwell be given a chance to escape.

These terms were accepted. The man for whom she had sacrificed so much rode out of Mary's life forever.

Mary was imprisoned. She was dragged through the streets of Edinburgh like a common criminal. The lowest of her subjects reviled and spat upon her. The highest bullied and threatened her. At last the ill and friendless queen agreed to abdicate in favor of her infant son. She was then taken to the grim fortress castle on an island in the middle of Loch Levan.

But the beautiful Queen of Scots was not yet through. Within ten months she had charmed two of her jailers into aiding her escape from that seemingly escape-proof prison. Once Mary was free, six thousand brave highlanders flocked to her standard. For a few weeks hopes ran high. Then came the battle of Langside in 1568.

Mary's undisciplined troops suffered a crushing defeat. The queen became a hunted refugee in her own land. With a handful of loyal followers she made her way southward. Against their advice she crossed over the Firth to seek asylum from her cousin Elizabeth. She found imprisonment instead. For the next nineteen years—nearly half of her short life—she was to suffer the humiliations and persecutions of a hated and feared political prisoner. Elizabeth, however, preferred to call it "honorable custody."

Some of Mary's sufferings were undoubtedly her own fault. Repeatedly and foolishly she allowed her partisans to involve her in ill-conceived plots which bore only bitter fruit. But it was not entirely her fault that she became a rallying point for all the disaffected elements in Elizabeth's realm, Catholic or not. To those of her own faith, of course, she was the purest of martyrs.

Mary's personal charms were still a potent weapon—so potent, in fact, that she attracted some of Elizabeth's highest nobles to her cause. The powerful Duke of Norfolk lost his head for love of the Scottish queen. Even jailers fell under her spell so that they had to be changed frequently. She was moved from prison to prison. And each new place of confinement was grimmer—and farther from the border—than the last.

In vain did she write letters to Elizabeth, alternately pleading and demanding to be allowed to come to court and present her case. The answer was always the same. The Queen of England would not—could not—receive her cousin until she had been cleared of the charge of murdering her husband.

A strange trial was even held for this purpose. The evidence produced against Mary by her one-time nobles was damning. It consisted of letters and love poems allegedly written by the queen to Bothwell while Darnley was still alive. These were the famous "Casket Letters," and arguments have raged for centuries over their authenticity.

Mary, of course, pronounced them forgeries, but her denials were in vain. Elizabeth still refused to see her.

Mary remained a prisoner, and the years dragged by. The plots around the exiled queen grew ever bolder and more desperate. At last, in 1587, they became too bold. Now they aimed at nothing less than Elizabeth's death and Mary's assumption of the crown of England. What is more, Mary fell eagerly into a trap set by Elizabeth's ministers. The English queen now had positive proof that her cousin was aware of and personally involved in the murder plans.

The trial of Mary Stuart was completely illegal. She was neither allowed counsel to plead her case nor permitted to see the documents upon which the charges were based. Nor did she ever once admit the right of the court to try her, a crowned and anointed sovereign, at all. But the time was long past for such legal niceties. That court had been convened for only one purpose—to rid Elizabeth and her realm of the threat which hung over them.

Mary was duly found guilty of treason against the realm. The proud head that had once seemed destined to wear the triple crown of Scotland, France, and England was condemned to be laid instead on the executioner's block.

Mary was now in her mid-forties, no longer the bonny young queen for whom men were willing to risk their lives. Not even her own son, now ruling Scotland as James VI, would lift a finger to save her. The famous red hair was streaked with gray. The beautiful face was lined with sorrow. The once lithe body was crippled with rheumatism brought on by years of close confinement in damp and dreary prisons. But she was still every inch a queen.

The manner of her dying befitted her dual roles as queen and martyr. Courage she had always had. Now she added dignity and a sincere piety which touched the hearts of even her enemies.

She was denied even the comfort of a priest of her own faith. Only a special dispensation from the pope allowed her to administer the last rites to herself. To the Protestant preacher who exhorted her, she declared firmly that she had lived and would die a Catholic. When he attempted to pray for her, she drowned out his words with Latin prayers.

She was still praying, crucifix in hand, when, on February 8, 1587, the keen-edged sword descended.

News of Mary's execution set off a frenzied outburst of grief and anger in the Catholic world. Now, when it was too late to save her, Spain took action. The Spanish Armada was launched against England.

Launched too was a spate of legends about the "martyred" queen of Scots. Those legends persist even today, and they have almost succeeded in making a saint of the all too human woman who was Mary Stuart. She remains one of the most romantic figures in all history.

"In my end," ran her prophetic motto, "is my beginning."

CHRISTINA WHO RENOUNCED HER THRONE

# 12

# CHRISTINA:
# The "King" Who Ran Away

"I was born," wrote Christina in her memoirs, "covered with hair, and my voice was strong and harsh."

Whether for this reason, or because everyone so ardently hoped for a boy, an incredible mistake was made. King Gustavus Adolphus was informed that his queen, Maria Eleonora of Brandenburg, had indeed given birth to a son. The guns of Stockholm boomed forth the news that Sweden at last had a crown prince.

When Gustavus Adolphus learned the bitter truth, he swallowed his disappointment manfully. "Let us give thanks to God," he said. "I hope this daughter may be as a son to me." Then he chuckled and added, "She ought to be clever, since she has taken us all in."

Since all Sweden had welcomed her as a prince, her father determined to educate her as one. He was delighted that the two-year-old Christina showed no fear when first exposed to the roar of cannon. Instead she clapped her tiny hands in excitement and demanded more. Soon the little girl became a familiar sight at his side as he went about among his troops.

For Gustavus Adolphus was a warrior king. His military genius had led the Protestant armies to many victories in the Thirty Years' War. He had invented improved weapons for his armies. And this deeply religious champion of Lutheranism had brought his country from insignificance to take her place as a great power within his own lifetime.

Christina was only four when he presented her to the Estates as his heir. Holding the golden-haired child in his arms, he asked them to accept her as their ruler should he be killed. The occasion was the eve of his departure for another of his interminable campaigns. He also demanded that his mighty armies swear allegiance to her before he marched away.

He never saw his daughter again. The "Golden King" of Sweden was killed at the Battle of Lützen, November 6, 1632.

Six-year-old Christina was now Queen of Sweden.

The widowed Maria Eleonora, though beautiful, was a shallow-minded, flighty woman. She plunged into an orgy of grief. She wept day and night in black-hung apartments. Worst of all, she insisted that Christina share in this hysterical display of mourning. The child was rarely allowed out of her mother's sight.

Such a state of affairs was intolerable to a sensitive child. She learned to detest her foolish mother. Undoubtedly, this early experience contributed to the scorn in which she ever afterward held almost all members of her own sex.

"I like men," she declared, "not because they are men, but because they are not women."

The regents, of whom Maria Eleonora was *not* a member, rescued the young queen. The dowager queen was banished to a country estate, and Christina's entire life was changed. Her long hair was cut short. She was dressed in boy's clothes. And the princely education prescribed by her father was begun in earnest.

Grizzled warriors taught her military strategy. Stern tutors drilled her in history, mathematics, science, and diplomacy. By the time she was fourteen she could speak and write Greek, Latin, Spanish, Italian, Dutch, French, and German as well as her own native tongue. Less successful, as we shall see, were those who tried to teach her the arts of finance and the obligations of a monarch. But that was not because of any lack of ability.

Christina was highly intelligent—a genius, in fact. "I had," she wrote, "an insatiable desire for knowledge." She read constantly and argued happily with every scholar who came her way. The brilliant Jean Dominique Cassini, who taught her astronomy much later, had this to say of his pupil. "It is a pity that so fine a mind should have been wasted on a queen and a woman. Had Her Majesty been born a male, she would have become one of the greatest scientists of this or any other age."

But Christina was by no means a bookish prig. She delighted in violent physical exercise. She was an excellent fencer, a deadly shot with musket and pistol, and the finest horsewoman in all Sweden.

No day was ever long enough for all the things that Christina wanted to do. Her energetic schedule exhausted those around her. No courtier, of course, might rest while the queen was up and busy. Nor could they indulge themselves in other ways. Christina was abstemious in all things. She ate little, seldom drank strong wines, and slept very little. She herself said that she devoted only three hours a night to slumber. Others disagree, but admit that it was rare for her to sleep more than five hours.

Vain and arrogant, she thoroughly enjoyed the attention all Europe focused upon her. Such attention was not without reason. This amazing girl queen readily grasped the complexities of statecraft and military strategy. She could discuss both intelligently with her ministers at the age of ten. At fifteen she regularly attended the meetings of her senate. And her advice carried much weight once it was realized that she was nearly always right. Her armies proved so successful that the Baltic soon became virtually a Swedish lake.

On her eighteenth birthday, Christina took the solemn oath as *King* of Sweden. Among other things, she swore always to uphold the Swedish Lutheran Church of which she was now the head.

Christina had undeniable talents as a ruler. She revised the tax system so that nobles and clergy should pay a fair share and relieved the peasants of the full burden they had carried. She encouraged exports that boosted the

Swedish economy. She liberally subsidized the guilds of artisans so that Swedish weavers and masons and woodworkers might compete fairly with those of other countries. Sweden, emerging abruptly from the Dark Ages, knew unparalleled prosperity under her rule.

Perhaps her most lasting reforms were in the field of education. To the learned queen, it was unbearable that she should reign over a nation of barbarians. Her father had founded the first university in Sweden. But it was Christina who lavishly endowed it and imported scholars from all Europe to staff it. She also gave a large tract of crown lands to establish another seat of learning at Uppsala. Nor was higher education her only concern.

An edict of 1649 made education available to every person in her land. Primary and secondary schools were established everywhere and generously subsidized by the crown. Also—an unheard of thing—*girls* were admitted freely if they showed ability to learn. Those who could not benefit from higher schooling were encouraged to learn useful trades. Thus did Christina establish an educational pattern for Sweden which still endures after three hundred years.

But on the whole, domestic politics bored the queen. She loved to dabble in all foreign intrigues. But her diplomacy had only one major aim. Christina longed for peace.

She yearned to see the Swedish court a center of art and learning. She hungered to be known as a patroness of all the muses. Yet nothing could be accomplished as long as the tiresome war dragged on and on. Christina signed a peace treaty with Denmark in the first year of her reign. She then poured her tremendous energies into negotiations for peace on the continent. It is largely due to her efforts that the Treaty of Westphalia was signed. The Thirty Years' War was over at last!

It was the one great diplomatic triumph of her life.

Christina's dream of a glittering court was at least partly fulfilled. Her reputation as a scholar attracted some of the most brilliant minds of the day. Among them was the great Descartes. His death while in Sweden was unfortunate, for there were many ready to lay the blame at the queen's door. He would have lived, they said, had she not forced him to conform to her own severe schedule.

The question of her marriage remained a constant source of irritation. Suitors, of course, were not lacking for such a matrimonial prize. Not only would she bring a kingdom as a dowry, but Christina of Sweden was, by all reports, incredibly beautiful. "Men who have seen her for the first time," wrote the French envoy to Stockholm, "when she appears in all her glory invariably fall in love with her."

Several Danish princes, the Elector of Brandenburg, and the kings of Hungary and Spain sent proposals. Her own cousin, Charles Gustavus, was considered a likely candidate. There even seems to have been a slight case of puppy love between these two. But that was before the queen's eye fell with favor on the handsome Magnus de la Gardie.

Characteristically, Christina had already made up her mind.

"I would rather die than be married!" she declared. "No one in heaven or earth can constrain me to it!"

She had a ready argument for those who insisted she must provide an heir for the throne. "I am as likely to give birth to a Nero as an Alexander." But she promised, if she married at all, that she would choose Charles Gustavus.

And she willingly signed an act of succession which named him as her heir. That, as far as Christina was concerned, settled the matter.

On October 20, 1650, Christina made a long-delayed formal entrance into Stockholm for her coronation. The lovely, flaxen-haired, blue-eyed queen was arrayed in magnificent ermine robes of state. She rode through the streets in an elegant black-and-gold carriage to the cheers of her enchanted people. They adored her despite the ruinous expense of this coronation. It had all but exhausted the treasury. For Sweden was already drained dry by pilfering regents, years of incessant wars, and Christina's own lavish spending.

Unfortunately, though Christina accepted their adoration as her due, she never really cared much for her land or her people. Already she was making other plans.

In 1651, the queen fell ill. The diagnosis of her physicians was overwork. That same year a tragi-comic incident occurred as she inspected a new battleship in the harbor. The admiral who was escorting her lost his balance. In his panic, he made a grab for the queen and succeeded in pulling her into the icy waters with him. Both were nearly drowned.

Perhaps Christina began to feel that wearing a crown was too dangerous as well as too burdensome. At any rate, it was about this time that she began to hint that she would like to abdicate. This brought such a storm of protest from both senate and populace that she hastily retreated, but by no means surrendered.

"Whatever I do," she compained, "it seems that Sweden will be ruined."

Her behavior, which had long been capricious, now

worsened. Her impulsive acts, her wild extravagance, her complete disregard for her own dignity shocked the nation. Her popularity waned until there were many in the land who wholeheartedly wished they were rid of her.

It was religion that forced the final decision. Christina had never been noted for her piety. Her habits of playing with her dogs or reading Greek and Latin texts during services had long scandalized the pious Swedes. Now this daughter of the great king who had fought and died in the cause of Lutheranism began to lean toward the detested Church of Rome. The pope sent disguised missionaries to fan the flames. But he scorned her offer to become a Catholic if he would allow her to take Lutheran Mass once a year.

"In that case, I must renounce the throne," she said.

Christina pleaded other reasons to her senate. "The King of Sweden," she pointed out, "should be able to lead his armies."

Actually, Christina was convinced she could lead an army as well as any man. Nor, let it be said, was religion more than an excuse for her abdication. She was, quite simply, bored to tears with the pomp and pageantry of her royal prison. She was weary of the burdens of queenship. She yearned to be free—to travel—to see the world she had thus far known only in books.

The Act of Abdication was signed June 6, 1654, in a moving ceremony. The noble whose duty it was could not bring himself to remove the crown which had been Christina's since infancy. Without hesitation she removed it herself.

It was her last act as a reigning monarch.

Charles Gustavus was crowned that same day. Christina left Uppsala in a downpour of rain that evening. Fearing that she might be prevented from leaving the country, she cut her hair short and donned the clothes of a boy. Accompanied by only four of her gentlemen, she rode with pistols at her waist into Denmark. As "Count Dohna" she traveled onward in this disguise.

One incident of the journey smacks of musical comedy. The Queen of Denmark, overcome with curiosity, wanted to see Christina. But she could not do so as a queen. She therefore disguised herself as a serving maid in the tavern where "Count Dohna" was staying. Christina soon learned who was waiting on her at table. With characteristic insolence, she devoted the entire meal to making unflattering remarks about the Danish queen.

Christina's first destination was Brussels. Her "personal" belongings had been sent ahead. They included a fabulous art collection and a priceless library which were really the property of the Swedish crown. Her former subjects were appalled by her casual appropriation of so much of their treasure. But there was worse to come.

Christina renounced her Lutheran faith and accepted Catholicism at Brussels. Nothing she could have done could have dismayed her former subjects more. But Christina did not care. She had traded her throne for the freedom to behave as she pleased.

There would be many moments in the next thirty-five years when she bitterly regretted that bargain.

The first years were exciting enough even for the adventure-starved queen. (She always retained the title and many of the privileges of a crowned monarch.) Her progress through Europe to Rome was a triumph. Catholic cities along the way vied to do her honor. And many an illustrious dignitary hastened to do her homage.

Christina entered Rome accompanied by eight princes of the Church. Wildly enthusiastic crowds lined her way. But even on so solemn an occasion as her first meeting with the pope, this unorthodox woman could not resist shocking everyone. She scorned the carriage the pope had sent for her. Instead, she rode a pure-white stallion. Her bridle and stirrups were of solid gold. Her saddle and reins were covered with cloth-of-silver. Her mannish cloth-of-gold blouse was open at the throat.

Worst of all, she rode astride. And though they were elaborately embroidered with gold lace, the garment that decked her lower limbs was definitely and scandalously a pair of breeches!

The sight of his royal convert kneeling at the high altar in such outlandish garb cannot have failed to dismay Pope Alexander. Nevertheless, he administered the sacrament with his own hands. And afterward he entertained the queen at a state banquet. To break bread with the pontiff was an unheard of honor for a woman!

The rest is anticlimactic.

By her giddy actions Christina alienated the Roman society which had welcomed her so warmly. She amused herself by dabbling in intrigues. She kept all Europe agog with her extravagance. She traveled restlessly, wearing out her welcome at every court. Often her journeys were undertaken without women attendants, and she wore masculine attire.

At Rome, she kept a brilliant salon for high churchmen,

artists, and scholars. She caused a riot in Hamburg by tricking the staunchly Protestant nobles into celebrating a Catholic fete. She even delved deeply into the forbidden "science" of alchemy.

Twice, she made bids to place another crown on her head. She entered into an intrigue to take over the kingdom of Naples with the help of France. And she offered herself as a candidate for election to the vacant throne of Poland. Both plans were ill-conceived and unsuccessful.

She even feuded intermittently with the Church. "Since I have been at Rome," she announced acidly, "I have seen four popes, not one of whom had common sense.

In 1657 came the scandal that rocked the world. It took place at Fontainebleau when she was a none-too-welcome guest of France. Christina became convinced that one of her attendants, a rascal named Monaldeschi, was a traitor. She confronted him with the evidence, obtained a confession, and sentenced him to death. To the autocratic queen it was no more and no less than an act of simple justice. She had always retained the power of life and death over her own small court in exile.

What made the business so unacceptable was the fact that the execution took place in the residence of her host. And it was so badly bungled as to amount to sheer butchery. Christina might call it justice, but the world condemned it as murder. She was invited to leave France, and the incident thoroughly blackened an already soiled reputation.

Throughout the years of exile, Christina's main concern was the mundane one of securing her promised revenues from her former kingdom. The queen's lavish scale of living insured that every penny was spent long before it was due. It was not only her own extravagance that kept her in debt. Her most trusted attendants consistently stole whatever they could lay their hands on.

Naturally, Sweden was not very eager to pay out the enormous sums required to support its absentee monarch. More than once she was forced to return to her homeland and press her claims in person. Each time her appearance aroused enthusiastic demonstrations among the people. They seemed to have forgotten her faults and they never ceased to love her. But each time she was assisted out of the country as quickly as possible. Finally, she was forbidden to enter the land she had once ruled.

But even so fiery and restless a spirit as Christina's must bow to the passing years. Gradually, she slipped into a quieter way of life. Her last violent quarrel with a pope began in 1677. It lasted two years and ended with a victory of sorts for the queen. It was her last battle.

The last ten years were quietly spent. Christina seemed finally to have really accepted the religion for which she had given up a crown. She contented herself with pious and studious pursuits. Artists, poets, and men of science flocked to her small court. Here they invariably found understanding and encouragement. She herself turned writer, producing a book of wise sayings as well as her incompleted *Memoirs*. The humiliations of a lifetime were forgotten, the sins forgiven.

Christina died in April, 1689.

The church bells of Rome tolled solemnly for twenty-four hours to mark the passing of Catholicism's most illustrious convert. Against her express wishes, she was buried with the pomp which befitted a reigning queen. Her elaborate tomb may still be seen in the Basilica of Saint Peter's in Rome.

One cannot help thinking it a strange resting place for this "Minerva of the North." She had, after all, once been the spiritual head of a militantly Protestant realm.

MARIA THERESA OF AUSTRIA

# 13

# MARIA THERESA:
## Mother of Her People

The great and powerful Hapsburg dynasty that governed Austria, Hungary, Lombardy, Bohemia, and a large part of the Netherlands produced many a ruler in its long history. Some were noble and good. Others were weak and incredibly bad sovereigns. But every one was, first and foremost, a Hapsburg to his aristocratic fingertips.

The infant daughter born to the Emperor Charles VI in 1717 was no exception. Maria Theresa Walburga Amalia Christina may very well have been the best of the lot. Still, she was destined to display every virtue and every failing of her clan during a reign which lasted nearly forty years.

Her training for the throne began at an early age. Despairing of a son, the emperor saw to it that the young archduchess was carefully instructed in the responsibilities which would one day be hers. Never was she allowed to forget her duty to her family and her people. Never was she allowed to enjoy anything resembling a normal girlhood.

Perhaps the only bright spot in her private life was her marriage at the age of nineteen to her cousin, Francis of Lorraine. It was, to be sure, a dynastic match. Nevertheless, Maria Theresa had the incredible good fortune to be truly in love with the man duty compelled her to accept as a husband.

The union was a happy one and remained so for twenty-nine years. Francis and Maria Theresa fulfilled their first obligation to the dynasty magnificently. Sixteen children were born in quick succession. Unfortunately, eleven of them were girls. And, though most inherited their mother's physical beauty, few displayed either her intelligence or her integrity.

Charles VI died when his daughter was twenty-three and he left her sole ruler of his mighty empire. Maria Theresa was a wise and capable woman by this time, but she was not aggressive. Her one desire was to pass this vast inheritance on to her sons intact. It was a task that would prove to be far from easy.

Almost before the young queen had seated herself on the throne, plots were afoot to snatch it from her. Fleury, minister to Louis XV of France, was preparing a plan for the partitioning of Austria. Frederick the Great of Prussia fairly drooled at the prospect of enlarging his paltry kingdom at the expense of a young and inexperienced woman. Every petty German princeling made a grab for a slice of the political cake. All this despite the fact that they had each solemnly sworn to uphold the Pragmatic Sanction. This was a formal statement recognizing Maria Theresa's rights to the possessions of the Austrian Hapsburgs.

The new queen saw great chunks of her territories wrested from her grasp. Frederick even had the audacity to propose that she give him disputed Silesia. In return he promised to support her husband's bid for the vacant post of Holy Roman Emperor. Maria Theresa refused indigantly, and Francis was elected without Frederick's help. Silesia, however, was lost in the war that broke out soon after.

Only her courage and statecraft saved Maria Theresa from worse losses. Prussia had formed an alliance with France against her—a seemingly unbeatable combination. Surrounded by her children, the lovely young queen made a dramatic appeal to her Hungarian Parliament. She begged for support in her struggle to keep what was rightfully hers. In return, she promised the Hungarians a large measure of self-government.

Fired with patriotic fervor, they granted her the men and money she so desperately needed. Maria Theresa used them wisely. She also took clever advantage of the frequent quarrels between Frederick and Louis. She found that she could play one against the other in her gamble for time. As a last resort, she entered into an unpopular alliance with England.

France, though tottering, was still the greatest power in Europe. And English promises were not the most dependable of weapons. Still, Maria Theresa had no choice but to tread the treacherous pathways of international intrigue. Elisabeth of Russia was her only dependable ally, for Elisabeth hated Frederick even more cordially than Maria Theresa did.

Silesia was the bribe that kept Frederick from further attacks, at least for a while. Maria Theresa used the respite to drive the usurpers from her thrones in Bavaria and Italy. By 1748, in fact, she had managed to regain possession of all her lands. The War of the Austrian Succession was over.

Maria Theresa had won. The "helpless" woman had proved herself quite capable of defending her fabulous realm. And she had done it without impoverishing that realm. This amazing queen had carried on eight years of bitter warfare during which her very survival as a reigning monarch was at stake. Yet her careful management had assured that her treasury, left empty by her father, was now filled to overflowing.

Eventually the Austrian hatred of Russia and distrust of England forced Maria Theresa to seek an alliance with France. She herself claimed that this was the one act of her life of which she was ashamed. For to gain her ends she had to stoop to making an intimate of the infamous Madame de Pompadour, mistress to Louis XV and virtual ruler of France. Through her, a marriage was arranged between the young Archduchess Marie Antoinette and the future Louis XVI.

The empress could not, of course, forsee the tragic fate which awaited her child. However, she certainly knew that Marie Antoinette had little chance of happiness at the French court. The problem of arranging suitable and advantageous matches for her ten surviving children earned Maria Theresa the title of "the greatest marriage broker in Europe." She was by no means unfeeling. In fact, she was an unusually devoted and loving mother. Still, the creed that had been instilled in her from childhood required that the individual be sacrificed for the good of the state—or of the family, which amounted to the same thing.

Ironically, the French alliance so dearly bought did Austria little good. Still, it must be counted as one of Maria Theresa's few diplomatic triumphs. The rather hollow title she wangled for her husband was another. Besides, it relieved her of one worry. Maria Theresa had realized early in her marriage that her own judgment was far superior to that of Francis. Consequently, she had steadfastly refused to allow him to interfere in any way between her and her people. Perhaps she did not plan it that way, but there is no doubt that being hailed as Holy Roman Emperor soothed Francis' pride and made things much easier for his wife. The queen was the first to proclaim the formula, "Long live the Emperor Francis I!"

Maria Theresa's record in domestic affairs is much better. There is no doubt that she earned the right to be called the "Mother of Her People." Among other things, she reorganized the tax structure to require nobles and clergy to assume a fair share of the burden. She established crown courts to see that her laws were equitably applied. She encouraged agriculture, industry, trade, and art. Best of all, she made education a concern of the state instead of the Church. Thanks to Maria Theresa, public schools were established throughout her realm.

When Francis died in 1762, Maria Theresa was plunged into terrible grief. She who had always been the best and most loving of wives indulged in an orgy of self-recrimination. She accused herself of neglecting her husband. She magnified his very virtue until he became, in her eyes at least, a far greater man in death than he had ever been in life. As a symbol of her mourning, she put away her jewels. Never again would the empress be seen in the dazzling array of a Hapsburg monarch.

Her oldest son, Joseph, succeeded his father as Holy Roman Emperor. He soon showed himself opposed to his mother's crafty and cautious foreign policies. Joseph admired Voltaire and adored Frederick the Great. His every effort was bent toward attaining an alliance between Austria and Prussia. His first meeting with the Prussian king in 1770 resulted in the shameful partition of Poland. That hapless country was to be carved up for the benefit of Russia, Prussia, and Austria.

Catherine of Russia regarded this as bad politics. Maria Theresa of Austria regarded it as nothing short of criminal. Still, as long as her Russian ally consented to that crime and her own son was one of the perpetrators, there was nothing the Austrian ruler could do to prevent it. Her old enemy, Frederick, sneered at her scruples.

"Maria Theresa," he said scornfully, "wept—and took."

But not even this partnership in crime could prevent

war clouds from gathering between the two nations. Once more Europe stood on the brink of an orgy of bloodletting. It was mainly through Maria Theresa's efforts that the impending tragedy was averted. The Peace of Teschen was signed in 1779. No other event in her long reign, Maria Theresa declared, gave her more satisfaction than this, her last diplomatic triumph.

It is as well that she did not live to see the terrible events of the next decade. They were to cost Marie Antoinette her life and inundate Europe in a sea of blood for nearly a quarter of a century.

Maria Theresa, Archduchess of Austria, Queen of Hungary, Queen of Bohemia, daughter, wife, and mother of Holy Roman emperors, died in 1780 at the age of sixty-three. She was the only woman in the long line of Hapsburgs ever to rule in her own right.

It is typical of the selfless devotion to what she conceived to be her duty that not even death could daunt her. The last hours of her life were spent in signing state papers and giving last-minute instructions to Joseph, who would succeed her.

Joseph urged his mother to save her strength, but she refused to spend the time still left to her in sleep.

"Are you at ease, Mother?" he asked.

"Sufficiently at my ease," the failing empress replied, "to die."

CATHERINE THE GREAT

# 14

# CATHERINE THE GREAT:
## Founder of Modern Russia

The world had little reason to take notice of an event which took place at Stettin in the spring of 1729. The birth of a daughter to Christian Augustus, Prince of Anhalt-Zerbst, and his wife, Princess Johanna Elizabeth of Holstein-Gottorp, went almost unnoticed.

Despite their high-sounding titles, the prince and princess were but petty members of the impoverished German nobility. He was a prince without a principality, she a princess without a fortune. They might have been—indeed they were—closely related to every royal house in

Europe. But that fact added nothing to the income Prince Christian derived as an officer in the Prussian army.

Nor did it guarantee social success for his child. Little Sophia Augusta Frederica, affectionately known as Figchen, grew up in an atmosphere of genteel poverty. She seems to have been a lively child, given to playing boisterous and tomboyish games with the children of Stettin. Of herself she was later to write, "My father, whom I did not see very often, believed me an angel; my mother took very little notice of me."

Her active mind and unquenchable curiosity, however, caused many of Figchen's relatives to consider her "impertinent." To add to her woes, she was not at all an attractive child. Under the circumstances, it did not seem likely that Princess Sophia would ever attract a prince of suitable rank.

She met young Peter Ulrich of Holstein at a family gathering in Kiel. She was ten at the time; he was eleven. Figchen thought the boy "really handsome, agreeable and well bred." He was her second cousin on her mother's side, already ruler of his own duchy and possible heir to both the Swedish and the Russian thrones. Small wonder that Figchen's ears pricked up when she heard family gossip coupling her name with his.

"Child that I was," she wrote in her memoirs, "the title of queen caressed my ears. . . . Gradually I grew accustomed to thinking myself destined for him." Nevertheless, such a marriage was a very remote possibility. It became even more so after the Empress Elisabeth formally accepted Peter as heir to the Russian throne.

Perhaps it was because no reigning king was willing

to sacrifice a daughter to Russian barbarism. Perhaps none could be found politically acceptable to the Russian nobility. Perhaps it was even because the empress was sentimental. She had once been betrothed to Johanna's brother. He had died before the wedding could take place, leaving Elisabeth prostrate with grief.

Whatever the reason, the miracle *did* happen. Johanna and her daughter received a peremptory summons to present themselves at the imperial court in Moscow. Elisabeth wanted to see for herself if this obscure fourteen-year-old princess would make a suitable wife for the Grand Duke Peter.

Sophia's father was a pious Lutheran. He raised some half-hearted objections to a match which would involve a change of faith for his daughter. Johanna was not nearly so fussy. She would have adopted Russian Orthodoxy herself to further her ambitious aims. Neither parent seems to have thought it any obstacle that the proposed bridegroom was rumored to be a liar, a craven, a bully, and at least half mad. Perhaps Sophia herself had no objection to marrying a "strange brute, streaked with insanity" if it brought her a crown.

So Figchen's meager wardrobe—three dresses, a dozen chemises, some stockings and handkerchiefs—was packed. The terrible midwinter journey to Russia was begun. Johanna was able to write enthusiastically of traveling in an imperial sleigh, "scarlet, decked with silver and lined with marten fur." Her daughter remembered only that her feet were so numb and swollen with the cold that she had to be carried from that luxurious sleigh at the end of each day's journey.

The first meeting with her future bridegroom was hardly encouraging. Peter took the opportunity to inform his cousin of his passion for a young lady of the court. Still, he seemed to like Figchen and professed himself ready to marry her if only to please his aunt. Sophia soon realized that it was Elisabeth she must win. In this, she succeeded very well.

The girl who aspired to the throne of Russia also knew that she must please the Russian people. To this end she accepted the Orthodox faith without a murmur. She also set herself the task of learning the language as quickly as possible. She would often sit studying for long hours clad only in a thin nightdress and exposed to freezing drafts. Consequently, she caught cold, and the neglected illness soon developed into pneumonia.

For days she hovered between life and death. The empress herself spent long hours at the bedside of the "adorable child." It did not harm the German princess' popularity when it was learned how she came to be ill. Nor did it hurt that she refused the services of a Lutheran minister, asking instead for a priest of her new faith. Such acts could not help but endear her to her adopted people.

Figchen recovered, but there were still delays. Elisabeth conceived a hearty dislike for the officious and demanding Johanna. There were times when it seemed as if both mother and daughter might be sent home in disgrace. The two children whose future was at stake had become genuinely fond of one another. Now they trembled at every threat of separation.

At last the formal betrothal was announced. The wedding was celebrated with great splendor in August of 1745.

Johanna was sent packing immediately after the ceremony. Sophia, now to be known as the Grand Duchess Catherine Alexievna, was alone in a foreign land. She would never set eyes on either of her parents again.

"The life I led for eighteen years," Catherine was to write, "would have been enough to make any ten people in my place go mad and twenty more to die of misery."

This may be exaggerated, but there is no doubt that the young couple suffered greatly. They were closely watched and heavily punished by the empress for the slightest indiscretions. They were kept virtual prisoners within their own household. Their attendants and servants were usually spies. Any courtier for whom the pair showed the slightest affection was promptly removed from his post.

Such persecution had the effect at first of drawing Peter and Catherine closer together. They became allies in their misery. Catherine neither died nor went mad. Her already unstable husband, however, was driven further and further into the dream world of insanity. Eventually, even the trust and affection he had felt for his wife turned to suspicion and hatred.

This strange marriage was childless for nine years. Then a son, Paul, was born. The child was immediately taken away from Catherine. She did not see him until he was six weeks old and seldom again after that. The empress herself would rear the boy. Soon everyone knew that Elisabeth hoped eventually to disinherit Peter in the child's favor. "My nephew, devil take him, is a monster," she wrote.

Catherine, married to that monster, had to accept the loss of her son without protest. For a long time she dared do nothing that might offend the empress. She buried herself in her studies and did everything she could to ingratiate herself with everyone. Only in the last years of Elisabeth's life did Catherine grow bold enough to dabble in the dangerous game of politics.

By that time it had become painfully obvious that Peter was unfit to rule. His hatred of his wife had reached the point where he talked openly of divorcing her. Catherine knew that she was loved as much as Peter was hated. But this only made her more of a threat to him. She feared for her life.

So, for that matter, did Peter, and not without cause. Catherine was quietly gathering support, and it was clear that there would be room on the Russian throne for only one of them. Only an accident prevented Catherine's party from making a move when Elisabeth died on Christmas Day, 1761. Peter, probably to his own surprise, was allowed to ascend the throne without incident.

He immediately embarked on a course calculated to alienate every segment of Russian society. He overthrew all Elisabeth's carefully planned foreign policies. He stopped the long war against Prussia, and forced his armies to adopt the hated Prussian uniforms. In effect, he offered Russia on a silver platter to the detested Frederick the Great. He earned the enmity of the Church by humiliating its clergy and confiscating its wealth. He drank himself into a permanent stupor with friends drawn from the dregs of humanity.

Worst of all, from Catherine's point of view at least, he insulted and threatened his wife on every possible occasion, public and private. As Catherine's brilliant biographer, Zoe Oldenberg, puts it, "Catherine scarcely needed to act at all; Peter was doing her work for her." In truth, his actions were those of a man bent on destroying himself. If this was his aim, he succeeded very well.

An attack of smallpox in adolescence had left Peter hideously ugly. Catherine, on the other hand, from an unattractive child, had blossomed into a very attractive woman. Though many flattered her, she was never vain. "To tell the truth," she confesses, "I never thought myself extremely beautiful, but I was pleasing, and I think this was my strong point." At any rate her name was linked romantically—and scandalously—with that of a handsome and swashbuckling officer of the Imperial Guard. It was with the aid of Gregory Orlov and his four officer brothers than she planned her coup.

Late in June, Peter made the mistake of moving to his summer palace and leaving his wife behind. On July 9, Catherine was at Peterhof, twenty miles from the capital. She was awakened by Alexei Orlov with the news that the time was ripe. She immediately set forth in a carriage drawn by borrowed horses to fulfill her destiny.

The Imperial Guard had been well primed with the vodka supplied by the Orlovs. Burning with hatred for Peter, they were easily persuaded to hail Catherine as empress. Within a few hours the entire populace had accepted the choice without a murmur. No doubt they felt that the devil himself would have been preferable to the infamous madman on the throne. Only a few German troops remained loyal to the fallen emperor and even these offered little resistance when Catherine rode out at the head of her army to take her husband prisoner and demand his abdication.

Peter abjectly submitted to arrest. He was dead nine days later, and Catherine denied all knowledge of his murder. That she was, in fact, innocent of the actual deed is almost certain. A letter found among her papers after her death places the guilt squarely upon Alexei Orlov. Nevertheless, Catherine was little grieved. Far from punishing her husband's killers, she showered them with honors and wealth.

Catherine was now ruler of all the Russias where legally she should have been only empress regent. She knew that many of those swearing allegience to her would have preferred to place the crown on the head of little Paul. Thus, when she did regain custody of her son, it was only to find him a threat to her own power. Furthermore, she was not allowed to forget for a moment just how she had gained that power. "The meanest soldier of the guard," she wrote, "thinks when he sees me that I am his work." The throne she had longed for was hers, but she would have to prove her right to keep it.

In the next thirty-four years she would do just that.

This German-born empress poured her amazing energies and talents into the task of making her adopted country great. She reorganized its trade. Imports doubled and exports tripled over those of Elisabeth's reign. She added territories amounting to nearly a quarter the area of European Russia to the realm. In the process she acquired outlets on both the Black and the Baltic seas. She constructed new cities and rebuilt and repopulated many that had fallen into decay. She colonized vast areas of new land and reorganized the administrative policies so that they might be centrally controlled. She doubled the size of her army and navy. She issued new laws designed to benefit her people.

It must be noted, however, that Catherine took no thought for the most wretched of all her subjects, the serfs. To her, of course, they were not subjects at all, but human cattle to be bought and sold. She treated her own reasonably well, but it would never have occurred to her to pass laws protecting those belonging to her nobles.

In addition to governing her huge country as an enlightened despot, Catherine found time to patronize the arts. She read avidly and kept up a voluminous correspondence with every important person in Europe. These included her hero, Voltaire. She also wrote numerous stories and plays which are, perhaps, best forgotten.

In short, Catherine took a backward and semibarbaric land and molded it into a nation which could take its place among the great powers of Europe. She took a disunited people and instilled in it the national pride which would allow her grandson, Alexander, to defeat the great Napoleon. And she earned for herself the title of "Catherine the Great."

Her private life was much less admirable. Her treatment of her son Paul was hardly that of a loving mother. She repeated with him many of the mistakes Elisabeth had made with Peter. She even deprived him of his children. The little Alexander was brought up under her supervision, and she doted on him. Only his refusal of the honor kept her from disinheriting Paul in his favor. But it was Alexander, not Paul, whom she always regarded as her heir.

Paul, in turn, cordially hated his mother. He openly declared that she was guilty of his father's murder. He idolized the dead Peter and imitated him in every possible way. He even ended up with a form of insanity more violent than his father had displayed.

However, it was in her scandalous love affairs that Catherine can be said to have done Russia a real disservice. With only one exception, she did not allow her favorites to interfere in her government. Still, her open-handed generosity to them is estimated to have cost the empire a total of eighty million dollars. Except for the Orlovs, few rendered any real service in return.

The one major exception was Gregory Potëmkin. He was a tall, black-visaged man with only one eye. He has been described as a knock-kneed, boisterous, unwashed, half-savage eater of garlic. Catherine, however, thought him extraordinarily handsome. He was also described as "nothing of a soldier and something of a coward." But he conquered the Crimea for her.

Potëmkin was among the young officers who helped to place Catherine on the throne. He served her faithfully all the rest of his life. But he also perpetrated one of the greatest hoaxes in history on her.

Catherine trusted her favorite with the most important posts in her government. To prove to her that the people were happy and loyal under his regime, he conducted the empress on a carefully planned tour. From her imperial barge, Catherine could see the dozens of charming villages that lined the river banks. When she landed she was greeted by gaily dressed, well-fed peasants who sang her praises—and Potëmkin's.

She had no way of knowing that the pleasant villages were only painted cardboard fronts. She could not see the same smiling "villagers" being hustled from place to place to greet her. She still did not know she had been tricked when Potëmkin died in 1791.

Catherine mourned him deeply as "my friend, almost my idol." Over and over she asked, "Whom can I rely on now?" And well she might, for Potëmkin more than any other had helped to make her reign great.

Catherine did not long outlive him.

For some time the great mind had been failing. The empress was tired of the long struggle. She was sick at heart over the terrible outrages of the French Revolution. There had been one stroke, almost as a warning, but she had recovered. The second came on November 10, 1796. Catherine never regained consciousness.

The people of Russia were plunged into deep and sincere mourning at the news. One of the few who did not weep was Paul, the new emperor. Still, not even his shabby trick of having Peter III's body exhumed and given the place of honor in a double funeral could humiliate her now.

Nothing could tarnish the bright legends which were already springing up to make holy the memory of Catherine, Little Mother of all the Russias.

QUEEN VICTORIA AND THE ROYAL FAMILY

# 15

# VICTORIA:
## Restorer of Monarchy

"That Alexandrina Victoria should ever have ascended the English throne," wrote a contemporary biographer "is perhaps the most remarkable event in her life."

This is a harsh judgment, and one not borne out by history. It does, however, point up the fact that the small daughter of the Duke and Duchess of Kent had few prospects. True, the infant princess born at Kensington palace on May 20, 1819, was technically fifth in line of succession. But her uncle George, who would soon be king, was still a young man. He could be expected to produce several heirs. Barring that, there was her uncle the Duke of York and his possible heirs and her uncle the Duke of Clarence and future children of his. Finally, there was her own father and the possibility of his sons.

Victoria, therefore, was not educated for the throne. Except for her parents' last-minute return from Europe (the money for the trip had to be borrowed) the future queen might not even have been born on British soil.

Victoria was only eight months old when her father died and her mother was left with only a small income to rear the little girl. The duchess kept Victoria close to her side, attending personally to every detail of the child's daily life and education. Not until she became queen did Victoria ever spend a night away from her mother's bedroom. Small wonder, then, that she threw off the rigid control when she got the chance.

In 1827 the Duke of York died without heirs. In 1830, King George IV followed him. King William, whose only children were already dead, sat on the throne. Miraculously Victoria stood next in line!

Immediately the education suitable to her high expectations was begun. By the time she reached her teens Victoria spoke French and German fluently. She could read Italian with ease and had translated the Latin classics. She showed a decided, and unexpected, talent for mathematics. History and geography, plus music, dancing, and art rounded out her studies. Of course the religious education of a future head of the Anglican Church was not neglected.

Victoria was not informed of what the future might hold for her until she was fifteen. Then her governess gave her a genealogical table of the English monarchs. Once it became clear that hers was the next name on the list, Victoria burst into tears. Then she dried her eyes and made the childish vow, "I will be good!"

That same year a cousin, four months younger than Victoria, came to visit. He was Albert Franz August Carl Emmanuel, second son of the Duke of Saxe-Coburg. He was destined to play an important role in the life of his fair cousin. Meanwhile, both had to grow up a little.

Victoria's eighteenth birthday was a national holiday. It was celebrated with particular fervor by the many enemies of the Duchess of Kent. Now she would never rule as regent for her daughter. Victoria had come of age.

And just in time. Four weeks later, at five o'clock in the morning, the Archbishop of Canterbury requested an audience. He came to inform her that King William was dead. The young Victoria was still in her dressing gown. She looked even younger with her hair streaming down her back. But she was now queen of the most powerful nation on earth. A few hours later she was holding her first cabinet meeting. Her sweet dignity made a favorable impression on the men who would govern in her name.

From the beginning the people took Victoria to their hearts. There would be times of strain in the coming years. But it is to the queen's credit that her people had no real cause to regret their genuine affection. She plunged eagerly into the business of ruling. Affairs of state intrigued her, so much so that she once wrote, "I *delight* in this work!" And she did. For one thing she was free at last.

If her relationship with her suave and charming prime

minister, Lord Melbourne, had a dash of the romantic in it, who can blame her? For a few short months scandal touched her name, but it is hardly surprising. She, who had never known a moment's freedom, was all too likely to become giddy with what she had attained so suddenly. But she soon put such things behind her.

Victoria was crowned with unprecedented pomp and splendor in June of 1838. The regalia of British kings proved a heavy burden for her frail figure. Already weighted down with crown and scepter, she asked what she was to do with the golden orb that threatened to break her wrist. She was told she must carry it in her hand. "Must I?" she asked, sighing. "It is very heavy." But her diary reveals that she loved every minute of the tedious five-hour ceremony. For it made her truly Queen of England.

Victoria enjoyed her freedom for the next year and a half. In November, 1839, she announced her engagement to the Prince of the many names, Albert of Saxe-Coburg. Actually, Victoria had done her best to dodge the issue of marriage. She had dreaded Albert's visit and tried to postpone it. Her diary reveals this and much more. On the night of his arrival she wrote, "Albert is *beautiful!*" Victoria was already in love.

Etiquette demanded that the queen propose to Albert. There is little doubt that she did so with a right good will, for she gave her heart with her hand. Very few queens have enjoyed that privilege. It was an extremely happy bride who stood at the altar in white satin and lace to exchange vows with the man she adored.

Albert *was* beautiful. He was also something of a dandy,

a bit more of a prig, and a great deal of a self-righteous bigot. Still, he was morally upright, devoted to what he considered his duty, and unswervingly loyal. He also possessed a talent, almost a genius, for organization and administration, and his policies were usually quite sound.

This was fortunate. Parliament was very careful to deny Albert any *legal* right to interfere in his wife's government. Nevertheless, for as long as Albert lived, his policies were Victoria's policies. He also bore the major burden of the tedious business of ruling.

It has long been held that Albert sacrificed himself on the altar of a loveless marriage. It is true that he was naturally very reserved. He cringed from any open display of affection and he was probably shocked by the emotional outburst in which his wife all too often indulged. It seems unlikely that he felt no affection for Victoria. No man is that good an actor. And Victoria never seemed to think that he was anything but a loving husband.

Certainly he did his duty as prince consort. He made the queen very happy, and he served England faithfully and well. The people, hostile at first, eventually learned to respect, if not to love him.

If the first duty of a sovereign is to provide heirs to the throne, then Victoria fulfilled that obligation royally. No less than nine sons and daughters were born in the short space of seventeen years. She has been described as "an exemplary mother of a family who was also an excellent queen."

Victoria's position in her government, however, was very different from that of the earlier queens. The monarchy had been gradually reduced in power until the crown was now little more than a headdress, and a tarnished one at that. The real business of government—the momentous decisions—was left to the ministers. Their sole obligation to the queen was to make sure that she understood their acts. She was expected to give her consent as a matter of course. Victoria balked once or twice. She crossed swords with the powerful Lord Palmerston in 1854. It was Victoria, not the prime minister, whom the people demonstrated against. War in the Crimea tended to bring queen and people together again, but it was a stormy period. Victoria had learned her lesson.

Time and again, Victoria found herself the target of a would-be assassin. The first time was in 1840. Two shots were fired at her from close range by a miraculously bad marksman. And other attempts followed. Somehow the queen always escaped injury when firearms were involved. She was knocked unconscious, however, and given an unqueenly black eye when a disgruntled Irishman attacked her with a cane. The usually heroic Victoria was very bitter about that incident. She considered it an unforgivable breach of etiquette.

Much as she adored him, it is strange that Victoria never saw that Albert was working himself to death in her behalf. His sudden collapse took her by surprise and his death in December, 1861, put her in a state of shock. Her grief was so terrible that it was feared she might go mad. The court was ordered into deep mourning. Victoria herself donned widow's weeds. She wore them the rest of her life.

For the remaining thirty-nine years of her reign she never again took up residence in London. Only seven times did she consent to come there for the opening of

Parliament. The people naturally resented the seclusion of one whom they considered more or less their property. They enjoyed, as they still do, the pageantry of royal appearances. It was even suggested that Victoria abdicate in favor of her eldest son. Victoria would have refused the suggestion even if she had not disapproved of Edward's conduct. Quite unfairly, she considered him partly responsible for Albert's death.

But if she failed in her showier duties, Victoria never failed to exercise her three rights as a constitutional monarch. These are the rights to be consulted, to encourage, and to warn. She was especially fond of that last one. She literally bombarded her prime ministers with warnings. Fortunately, after Lord Palmerston's death in 1865, she was served by competent ministers with whom she could work more easily.

Lord Russell, Gladstone (whom she detested), and Disraeli saw her through many a crisis. Disraeli completely charmed her. It was he who persuaded her to come out of her deep mourning and make an occasional public appearance. He attributed his success to one thing. He never, he said, disagreed or refused the queen anything, but he sometimes "forgot."

Reform bills and extensions of voting rights were passed. Irish home rule and reorgaization of the army became burning issues. The Suez Canal was purchased and India was added to the empire. Two wars were waged and Gordon was massacred at Khartoum. The Industrial Revolution brought its dizzying changes. All these thorny problems and many more were met during Victoria's reign.

The years 1880-1885 were particularly stormy. The

queen was constantly criticized, constantly bickering with her ministers. After that, imperialism became the watchword. Victoria, living symbol of the empire, took a maternal interest in all its varied peoples. The century drew toward its close with a period of unparalleled prosperity. Victoria was honored by her grateful subjects with the Golden and Diamond Jubilees of 1887 and 1897.

Victoria's life was also drawing to a close. She barely survived the century in which she was born. She died in January, 1901, respected, loved, and sincerely mourned by men of every race, creed, and color throughout the world. And no wonder. Victoria had found the British crown trampled into the dust by countless generations of mean and petty wastrel kings. She had lifted it up and worn it with pride and dignity. To her and her alone belongs credit for the esteem in which the British monarchy is held today.

So ended the longest royal lifetime in history and the longest reign in the annals of Great Britain.

Not only a queen had passed away. With her passed the bittersweet era that will always bear her name—the Victorian era.

# 16

# TZU HSI:
# The Old Buddha

She was born at the Hour of the Tiger on the Double Tenth (tenth day of the tenth moon) in the fifteenth year of the reign of the Emperor Tao Kuang. By the Western calender that was four A.M. on November 28, 1835. Her parents, though they lived in near-poverty in the old Tatar city in the northwest corner of Peking, were of proud lineage. The newborn infant could trace her ancestry back on both sides to the earliest Manchu rulers. The soothsayers who cast her horoscope the moment she was born predicted a brilliant future.

She would be known by many an exhalted title in her long life, but her mother called her Ta Ts'ui—Green Jade.

Green Jade, though small for her age, was an exceptionally beautiful child. She also possessed a forceful personality which made her the acknowledged leader of her playmates. Not that there was much time for play. Her unusual intelligence was quickly recognized. The rigorous demands of a classical education kept the child fully occupied from the age of four.

As Green Jade grew, the family fortunes improved. Her father, Hwei Cheng, worked his way up from minor government posts to hold ever-higher offices in several of the provinces. His moves took little Green Jade traveling over the sprawling Chinese Empire. She observed at first hand the people, the customs, and the problems peculiar to each region. She learned much of the machinery of administration by helping Hwei Cheng with the mountains of paperwork required of every Chinese official. Such lessons were to stand her in good stead later on, and she learned them well.

Then came tragedy and disgrace. Hwei Cheng fled his post in panic at the threat of a raid by fierce rebels who called themselves T'ai P'ing. Worse yet, he embezzled the official funds which were in his trust. Since the raid failed to materialize, this treachery was quickly discovered. He was caught and imprisoned, but he died before he could be brought to trail.

Green Jade and her mother beggared themselves to pay Hwei Cheng's debts. The little family returned to

Peking penniless. There they lived humbly, taking in sewing and mending to eke out a bare living.

Green Jade had never forgotten the glowing prophecies at her birth, but those dreams seemed hopeless now. The only chance to improve her lot had been the possibility that she might be chosen from among all the eligible Manchu maidens as a member of the imperial household—perhaps even to become the wife of the young emperor!

Now, her father's crimes almost barred her from the competition. Only the fact that Hwei Cheng had never actually been convicted kept her from being disqualified. But even when that danger was safely passed, there were others. For one thing, she had no money for the necessary finery in which to appear for the examinations.

Faithful friends provided the funds at the last moment. Green Jade passed the preliminary physical and mental examinations with flying colors. Now, all the loveliest candidates must pass the final test. One by one they were summoned before the throne so that the emperor himself might make his choice. When the names of those chosen to bear the title of Imperial Concubine were read out, Green Jade's was among them. But she had been the last chosen, not the first. Another would assume the coveted position of first wife and empress.

Green Jade was only seventeen when she went to live in the bewildering maze of lakes and gardens, palaces, pagodas, and temples that made up the Forbidden City. She plunged at once into the even more intricate maze of palace intrigue. Everything depended on her ability to find favor with the emperor. But her first move was to make a friend and ally of the powerful dowager empress.

Her second was to recruit a nucleus of faithful officials and servants who would become her personal espionage system. Both were wise moves.

Her early career was stormy. More than once she endangered everything by quarrels with the emperor. In time, however, her incredible beauty, amazing intellect, and driving ambition won out. She picked her way safely along dangerous paths to become the acknowledged favorite. And no wonder. Not only could this fascinating woman dream up an infinite variety of entertainments to while away the leisure hours; she could also help with the endless chores of government. The emperor was soon consulting her about his most important decisions. Imperial decrees were often drafted in Green Jade's exquisite calligraphy.

Her influence on the weak and vacillating emperor was enormous and, on the whole, good. When, in 1856, she also presented him with his only son and an heir to the throne, her position was assured. She had reached the highest position to which a Chinese woman could aspire.

But the affairs of the empire were going badly. China's age-old policy of excluding foreigners enraged the Western powers who hoped to exploit her. A small incident was seized upon as excuse for an invasion. The French and British marched in force against Peking.

In vain did Green Jade plead with the emperor not to flee. His health was delicate, and she knew there was a conspiracy afoot to kill her and the empress should he die under the rigors of exile. Since he was stubborn, she took what precautions she could. The court reached Jehol in safety. There, they received the imperious demands of the "foreign devils" who were ravaging Peking.

To Green Jade's dismay, the emperor granted them a huge indemnity and concessions which virtually opened the land to foreign conquest. These included the toleration and protection of the detested Christian missionaries.

But she had other, more immediate, problems. Her spies had told her that the emperor was failing fast. She was forcibly kept away from him by the conspirators. They also persuaded the dying man to sign a decree that would require Green Jade and the empress to commit suicide at the death of their lord and master.

Fortunately, such a decree was worthless unless it bore impressions from the imperial seals. And somehow those large, heavy objects of carved jade had disappeared.

Only after his death were the two women allowed at the Emperor's bedside. They found the fatal decree, still unsealed, under his pillow and destroyed it. But they were powerless to prevent the conspirators from declaring themselves regents for Green Jade's son, now the Emperor T'ung Chih. They could only maintain an air of grieving indifference until they could make good their escape.

Custom decreed that the bereaved widows meet the funeral procession at the gates of Peking. Here was her chance. Green Jade, taking the boy emperor with her, set out for the capital. It was a journey fraught with peril. Besides the usual dangers, an ambush had been set to kill her and kidnap T'ung Chih. With the aid of her cousin, Jung Lu, commander of the imperial guards, she escaped. Once safe in the Forbidden City, Green Jade wasted no time. The official seals—for of course it was she who had taken them—were put to good use.

By imperial decree, the Empress Tzu An and Green Jade, now known as Tzu Hsi, would share the regency for the young emperor. The conspirators, according to rank, were either executed or "allowed" to commit suicide.

Tzu Hsi soon showed herself the real power in the regency. She was only a woman, and very young besides, but she was probably the best qualified person in all China to manage the stricken empire. She was farsighted and quick to act in emergencies. She combined a rare intelligence with a truly astonishing grasp of the intricacies of statesmanship. The less ambitious Tzu An was reduced to the task of caring for the boy. T'ung Chih, quite naturally, learned to love her, while he actually feared his real mother.

There is an oddly persistent story to the effect that, unknown to Tzu Hsi, her co-regent possessed a decree from the dead emperor which could have ended her career at any time. If so, it is a mystery why Tzu An never used it. She always outranked Tzu Hsi, but she never exerted her power in any way.

Her one attempt to assert herself ended in complete humiliation. In the twenty-seven months preceding the official funeral of the late emperor, Tzu Hsi had consolidated her powers. Then Tzu An claimed precedence during the ceremonies. Tzu Hsi not only forced the empress to give way, but she threatened to remain at the tomb until everyone had apologized for the insult. Two weeks later court and empress made a four-day journey to make their apologies. No surer proof exists of just how indispensable Tzu Hsi had become—nor how very sure of herself she was.

So Tzu Hsi ruled the empire. Sitting in a veiled recess beside the golden throne, she passed down her judgments and decrees in an endless stream. No decision could be made without her authority; no matter was too small for her attention. Mountains of state documents were read and personally approved. Audiences started in the wee hours of the morning and decrees were drafted into the wee hours of the next. It was a staggering schedule for anyone, but Tzu Hsi seemed to thrive on it.

The years slipped by until T'ung Chih was suddenly grown and ready for marriage. Against his mother's wishes, the beautiful and intelligent Aluteh was chosen for him. Aluteh encouraged her husband to defy Tzu Hsi, and the young couple were forcibly kept apart. Tzu Hsi had no right to do this. Her son was now officially of age and the regency at an end. But Tzu Hsi never allowed him more than the semblance of power. She even seems to have developed a dislike of her son.

As a result, T'ung Chih sunk deeper and deeper into the depraved way of life which undermined his health and brought a tragically early death. He left no heir. Traditionally, it should have been Aluteh, now dowager empress, who adopted a child to sit on the throne. Such an action would have relegated Tzu Hsi to the powerless position of grand empress dowager. This was unthinkable, of course.

Tzi Hsi solved the problem neatly. She adopted her own nephew, four-year-old Tsai T'sien, and blandly assumed the regency for him. None dared oppose her, though she outraged established convention. The only person brave enough to try was Aluteh. For her pains, she was forced to commit suicide by "eating gold"—actually a compound of mercury.

Relations with Tzu An, too, had been getting worse for some time. Perhaps, as was whispered, Tzu Hsi at last discovered the existence of that fatal decree. Perhaps she simply grew tired of keeping up the pretense of deferring to her sister regent. There is even the possibility that Tzu An actually did fall victim to some swift and deadly disease. The only certainty is that the dowager empress died in agony shortly after eating a gift of rice cakes sent her by Tzu Hsi.

Tzu Hsi was fifty-five when Tsai T'sien came of age. Reluctantly she handed over the government and retired to her fabulous summer palace. Actually she had made him promise publicly that he would do nothing without her approval. So the real power was still in her hands when she chose to use it. A plot to overthrow her in 1898 provided the necessary excuse to resume control openly.

She now turned energetically to meet the growing foreign threat. Chinese hatred of the Westerners was not groundless. European powers gathered at her borders like jackals to wrest her empire from her. Already France had taken Indo-China. Japan had seized Korea. Britain had grabbed Burma and Russia laid claim to Mongolia. Small wonder, then, that Tzu Hsi initially encouraged the fanatic bands of the religious sect which became known as the Boxers. Their avowed aim was nothing less than death to all foreign devils.

Only the influence of her wiser ministers and of Jung Lu, now her commander-in-chief, saved every white person in China from being massacred. The death toll ran high enough as it was. It also provided ample provocation for another invasion.

Peking fell once more, and the imperial court went into exile. The empress herself was forced to flee in the dress of a peasant woman. She endured incredible hardships on the journey to Sian Fu. From there, she was able to negotiate a peace which was, on the whole, favorable. The haughty Westerners could not know that she herself had already decided on many of the reforms they had forced upon her.

In October, 1901, the court was able to return to Peking. The empress greatly enjoyed the last stages of the journey. She daringly trusted herself to the mercies of that fire-breathing iron dragon, the railway train. It was a fine homecoming.

Her people greeted her with loyalty and enthusiasm They had long forgiven her the illegality of her reign. The emperor, though no longer a prisoner, had renounced all pretense of power. She now accepted foreign interference as inevitable and set herself to charm the European ambassadors. She even received the detested whites socially. She allowed her portrait to be painted by an American woman to be given as a gift to the United States. In return, the foreigners openly respected and admired her.

The later years of the reign were marked with ever-increasing contacts with the outside world. Sweeping internal reforms and ambitious building programs kept her busy at home. Among the latter was her own magnificent tomb. Elaborate celebrations commemorated the seventieth birthday of the "Old Buddha," as she liked to be called.

Four years later, illness forced her temporary retirement.

While she was recuperating at the summer palace, a terrible omen appeared. A fiery orb traversed the night sky and sent the entire court into a frenzy of superstitious terror. It was only a comet paying its regular visit. But it was a thoroughly shaken Tzu Hsi who returned to Peking. Nor, it would seem, were her fears completely unjustified.

She had come back to receive an important state visit by the revered Dalai Lama of Tibet. At a banquet in honor of the distinguished guest both the empress and the emperor were taken violently ill. Tzu Hsi received the best of care and soon rallied. But Tsa' T'sien, alone and virtually unattended, was dying, and none dared tell her of his plight.

When she finally learned the truth, Tzu Hsi wasted no time but adopted yet another infant. This time it was her own great-nephew, Jung Lu's grandson, who became heir to the throne. The forgotten emperor was found dead next morning, but the Manchu dynasty was safe.

Tzu Hsi realized that she would soon follow the same path. She suffered remorse. Over and over she repeated, "I have made many mistakes." She trembled in fear of retribution for her many crimes. She seemed convinced that she had also failed as a ruler, an opinion with which historians do not agree.

"I have sinned enough," she moaned. "I shall die." And she added, "Never again make a woman regent and ruler of China."

And so, in August, 1908, Tzu Hsi died.

She was buried with imperial honors as was her due. Her robes were stiff with gold, crusted with jewels. Her great coffin was richly inlaid and lacquered in yellow, the color of royalty. And buried in her tomb were treasures valued at $750,000,000.

Such fabulous wealth, of course, practically guaranteed that the tomb would be looted. It was—not once, but twice. After that there was nothing to replace the treasures. The Manchu dynasty, which had been kept on the throne so long by her indominitable will, had fallen. The little boy who had been her last choice for the throne was a powerless prisoner.

Today, the tomb is virtually empty. All that remains is the magnificent lacquered coffin in which the great empress still sleeps. But now she is dressed only in the unadorned blue robes of a simple Manchu woman.

QUEEN WILHELMINA GREETING HER PEOPLE
FROM THE PALACE BALCONY, AMSTERDAM

# 17

# THE
# NETHERLANDS QUEENS:
## A Feminine Dynasty

With eight illustrious Williams among her ancestors, it seemed only fitting that the little princess of the House of Orange should bear the name of Wilhelmina. She was born at The Hague on August 31, 1880, the only child of sixty-three-year-old King William III of Holland and his second wife, Emma of Waldeck-Pyrmont. There were two older half-brothers, both of whom died within a few years. Little Wilhelmina was joyfully hailed as heiress to the throne.

Childhood at the royal palace of Het Loo offered many

charms. There were rabbits and chickens and a small donkey for pets. There was a little flower garden all her own. There were swings and seesaws and ponds for sailing toy boats. There was even an elegant little Swiss chalet with furnishings and dishes in little-girl scale and a tiny kitchen where one could really cook. And, when she was big enough, there was a team of four Shetland ponies, a gift from the king. These she learned to drive four-in-hand around the park in her little wicker pony cart.

What there was *not* was another child with whom a little girl might share these treasures. Queen Emma did her best. She took the child for drives and told her Bible stories. As long as his health allowed it, King William set aside an hour each day to be with her. They had wonderful times together.

But the king fell ill when Wilhelmina was only seven and was only rarely well enough to see her. Not only did she miss him, but the strain of a household geared to illness depressed and disturbed her. When death came at last, the terrible black-draped mourners she must now receive frightened her. Through her own grief, she knew that she was now the queen. But she did not at all understand what that title entailed. How could she? She was only ten years old.

The quiet life of Het Loo gave way to the even more circumscribed one of the court. Queen Emma was made regent and set herself seriously to the task of educating Wilhelmina as queen as well as future head of the Dutch Reformed Church. The little girl was set to work learning arithmetic, geography, Dutch history, and several languages. Piano lessons were tried, but Wilhelmina had no ear for music. Nor did dancing appeal to her. Art lessons, however, were a great success. Wilhelmina loved to sketch and paint, and she showed no little talent. This was encouraged, and she found satisfaction from this hobby all through her life.

There were some official duties even when she was still very young. The burden became increasingly greater as the years passed. In her autobiography, Wilhelmina referred to her life as "the cage." Always she longed for just a little of the freedom other children enjoyed. But a queen is never free.

On her eighteenth birthday, Wilhelmina came of age. Her reign now began officially. She was installed with impressive ceremony and drove through the streets to cries of "Long live the Queen." She seems to have been surprised that, once this flurry of excitement died down, life in the royal palaces went on much as before.

In the summer of 1900 she took a holiday with her mother at a mountain resort in Germany. There she met for the second time in her life young Hendrick of Mecklenburg-Schwerin. This time she promptly fell in love with him. Within a few months she was happily planning the wedding, which took place in February, 1901.

It was a happy marriage. The young couple soon settled into the uneventful routine of their lives. Wilhelmina still chafed against the bonds of convention that held her. She bitterly resented the fact that, no matter what she did, some segment of Dutch society felt called upon to criticize her. She was bored with being a ruler who was not allowed to rule. Even the joys and fulfillment of motherhood were long denied her. It was eight years before her only child, Juliana, was born.

The tragic events of World War I and the struggle to maintain the tenuous neutrality of her small nation gave Wilhelmina her first taste of the burdens of monarchy. It also gave her the chance to rid herself of some of the tedious ceremonies and unneccessary servants that had plagued her for so long. At last her potential as a leader of her people was being realized. The bars of the cage were pushing outward ever so little.

Best of all, she found a chance to do what she had always wanted. She could go about among the people. She could talk to them as one human being to another, and she loved it. This condescension on the part of royalty horrified some, but it endeared her to most. This was dramatically proved soon after the war. Certain elements tried to capitalize on the general unrest to overthrow the monarchy.

Loyal Dutchmen then gathered at The Hague in thousands to express their allegiance to the queen. When Wilhelmina appeared, they unhitched the horses from her carriage and fought one another for the privilege of drawing the heavy vehicle through the streets. Similar heart-warming demonstrations were repeated throughout Holland.

The postwar years were filled with activity. Holland and its queen were drawn willy-nilly into world affairs by membership in the League of Nations. And there were many domestic crises to be met. Nevertheless, Wilhelmina was able to renew her art lessons. Some of her happiest times were spent with Hendrick and Juliana on tours. They always chose places where the queen could paint Europe's magnificent scenery.

Double tragedy struck in 1934. The death of Queen Emma was closely followed by that of Hendrick. With

Juliana's help, Wilhelmina weathered her grief. Juliana's marriage in 1937 and the birth of the Princesses Beatrix and Irene were times for rejoicing. There were few such occasions in those years of gathering doom when Europe trembled before each crisis that brought war a step closer.

When World War II finally broke out, Holland once again declared her neutrality. But Adolf Hitler was no respecter of such formalities. The Dutch borders were overrun with terrifying swiftness. Juliana and her children were immediately sent to safety. Wilhelmina stayed on, hoping to remain at her post at The Hague.

Such hopes were soon dashed. The small Dutch army had no chance against the crack German troops that were pouring in. The queen took ship for still-unoccupied Zeeland, only to find it impossible to land. There was nothing to do but seek refuge in England. The government of her far-flung empire must be continued from exile.

Though it was much criticized, this was the only course open to her. Wilhelmina's realm consisted of far more than that small area now mostly in German hands. It was vital that Dutch citizens throughout the globe know that their nation, in the person of their queen, still existed. She could never risk falling into enemy hands as did the unfortunate Leopold of Belgium.

Juliana was sent to Canada in 1940, but Wilhelmina would flee no further. She sat out the Battle of Britain, often carrying her vital state papers with her to the air-raid shelter. She spoke frequently on the radio, offering what hope and comfort she could to a land enslaved by enemy occupation. She encouraged the free Dutch to do their utmost to aid the war effort. She established a center in

London for those fortunate enough to escape from occupied territories. Wilhelmina and the white flower she always wore became symbols of the Dutch underground resistance.

In 1941, Wilhelmina took her first airplane ride. An American plane whisked her across the Atlantic to visit Juliana in Canada. Later, she addressed the United States Congress and found time to visit a few historical sites. Then she winged back to war-torn Europe for another anxious three years.

It was not until 1945 that the Allies succeeded in liberating even a small portion of Holland. In March, Wilhelmina could return to her realm, though only for a brief visit. It was a dramatic moment when the queen's motorcade stopped at the border. A lone figure, an aging woman dressed in clothes that had been fashionable a generation before, descended and walked briskly across the line. Thus did the Queen of Holland return to her people.

Toward the end of April she could return to stay. By July 7, the queen was once again in residence at The Hague. "What an unforgettable journey it was!" wrote Wilhelmina.

But aside from the undeniable thrill of homecoming, there was little reason for rejoicing. Holland had been left a bleeding and devastated land. The work of reconstruction was slow and painful. Gradually, the valiant efforts of a courageous and determined people led by a no less determined and courageous queen brought order out of chaos. Holland took her place in the new Europe as a prosperous and—more important—a free nation.

By that time Wilhelmina was approaching her sixty-eighth birthday and the fiftieth anniversary of her reign. She was weary, and she now voiced her determination to abdicate in favor of her daughter. Only her characteristic desire not to disappoint her people kept her on the throne a little longer. She did not wish to deny them the great jubilee celebration they had planned.

On September 4, 1948, Queen Wilhelmina signed the papers which put an end to her reign. Then, exactly on the stroke of noon, she appeared on the balcony of The Hague to present to her assembled subjects their new monarch, Queen Juliana.

As Princess Wilhelmina, she lived quietly. Painting, gardening, embroidering, writing her memoirs, and enjoying the antics of four lively granddaughters were amusements enough for the next fourteen years. She died peacefully in her sleep on November 28, 1962.

An entire nation grieved as Wilhelmina's all-white funeral cortege passed through the streets. Surely there was not one in all that multitude who had lost more than Queen Juliana. The new queen had many reasons to be grateful to her mother's memory.

Wilhelmina had been determined to spare her child as much as possible from the cruel restrictions of "the cage." Juliana had grown up at Het Loo just as her mother had. She had ridden in the same parks and played house in the same Swiss chalet, but with an important difference. Wilhelmina saw to it that she did not play alone. Other children were invited to the palace regularly. The queen often put aside all but her most pressing duties to spend the golden summer days with her daughter.

Pets were encouraged and included horses, dogs—even

frogs. Once there was a fawn so young it had to be bottle-fed. Nor did this princess have to sneak away to learn to skate on the frozen pond as the other once did. Like tennis and sailing and bicycling and swimming, such activities were a normal part of her childhood.

When school time came, a class was formed which met at the palace. Juliana would know the healthy competition of children her own age. Only after it became apparent that she would inherit the throne were private tutors hired. She showed talent for music and willingly practiced on the violin, the instrument she chose. She also enjoyed choral singing with a group especially formed.

When she was old enough, Juliana went to summer camp and mingled freely with girls of many different backgrounds. In 1927 the eighteen-year-old crown princess was allowed to move into an apartment with three other girls and register as a regular student at the University of Leyden. This was an unheard-of thing for royalty.

Wilhelmina could not spare her daughter all the responsibilities of her rank, however. Nor did she try. Juliana was expected to make public appearances with her parents at an early age. She was taught the tiresome court etiquette along with the three R's. From eighteen on she was a member of the Council of State, and she accompanied her mother to the opening of the States General every year.

Her first independent action came with the forming of the National Crisis Committee to cope with the problems of the crippling depression of the 1930's. It was a mature Juliana who supported her grief-stricken mother through the tragic deaths of mother and husband.

Juliana now took her father's place as head of the Dutch

Red Cross. She began to represent the royal family at functions ranging from the World's Fair in Brussels to the Olympic Games in Bavaria. It was at the latter that she met Prince Bernhard.

Inevitably, there had been much speculation about Juliana's matrimonial future. She was rather plain, and romance had seemed to pass her by. Now she made up for lost time. But Bernhard's visits were kept secret at first. This was partly to avoid premature gossip. But the main reason was that the prince was a German, and the Germany of Adolf Hitler was extremely distasteful to the people of Holland.

The young man's background was thoroughly investigated, and he was pronounced free of Nazi taint. Still there was some unpleasantness when Juliana married Bernard on January 7, 1937. Most of the Dutch people, however, rejoiced with their radiantly happy princess as she set out on her four-month honeymoon.

Ten months after the wedding that happiness was almost snatched from her. Bernhard was seriously injured in an automobile accident. Juliana spent anxious days at his bedside before he was pronounced out of danger. Soon after Bernhard was released, Juliana became the patient, when the Princess Beatrix was born.

When the terrors of war burst upon Holland, there were two little girls to be hurried to the safety of England and later to Canada. Bernhard, of course, stayed behind to serve his adopted land. There were few visits. Juliana whiled away her exile by good-will missions to the United States and flying visits to some of the Dutch colonies. A third daughter, Margriet, was born in an Ottawa hospital room that had been officially declared Dutch territory for the occasion.

No such precautions were needed to make certain that the fourth princess was born a true Dutchwoman. Juliana had returned to her homeland. Without fuss she pitched in to help rebuild the stricken realm. In 1948 she quietly assumed the role for which she had been trained.

Juliana is, above all, her mother's daughter. The reigns of the two queens have been virtually a continuous one. True, the realm has shrunk since Juliana came to the throne. Most of the colonial possessions were given their independence in 1949. But the thriving economy of the homeland has not been seriously affected.

Juliana has accelerated the process of cutting through the tiresome ceremonial which once guarded all approaches to the throne. She makes herself accessible to her people. They, in turn, regard her as a sort of court of last resort—and a just one too.

Her children have been allowed the freedom Wilhelmina would never have dreamed of—possibly would never have approved of either. They attended progressive schools with the children of commoners. They are allowed to make their own decisions. Two crises have developed in recent years over marriage plans. Princess Irene wanted to marry a Catholic. Princess Beatrix chose another of the detested Germans. Both have married the men they chose.

Except for the most formal occasions Juliana looks, acts, and seems to regard herself as just another housewife. She has traveled extensively and entertained many distinguished visitors. But her shyness makes her prefer less formal surroundings than the palaces of her ancestors. Still, she can—and does—act the part of a true Queen of Holland when the occasion demands it.

It is hard to say what lies ahead for Juliana. There is much unrest abroad in the world and Holland has its share. But if the response of her people to Queen Juliana's combined fifty-third birthday and silver wedding anniversary is any indication, the foundations of the Dutch throne remain firm after seventy-five years of petticoat rulers.

ELIZABETH II – A GRACIOUS, MODERN
MONARCH

# 18

# ELIZABETH II:
## Thoroughly Modern Monarch

Elizabeth Alexandra Mary, daughter of the Duke and Duchess of York, was born April 21, 1926. At that time she was third in line for the throne of her grandfather, King George V, but it did not seem important. There was little fanfare over the arrival of the pretty, golden-haired princess.

Not that the nation did not take her to its heart. Her parents returned from a tour soon after her birth with four tons of extra luggage. This was toys presented by the people for the baby Elizabeth. And Elizabeth made them proud. She showed early signs of a superior intelligence and possessed a strong sense of duty even as a child. But she also had an enchantingly sunny disposition which made her the darling of everyone, doting grandfather included.

When she was four, a baby sister joined her in the nursery. Told that the new princess was named Margaret Rose, Elizabeth announced solemnly, "I shall call her bud. You see, she isn't a rose yet."

The two little girls were sheltered as much as possible against the glare of publicity. They actually led quiet and rather uneventful lives. Shortly before Elizabeth turned six, a governess was chosen for them. Marion Crawford, "Crawfie" to her charges, reported that King George had few requirements. "Teach them to write a decent hand," he told her. "That's all I ask."

Crawfie, of course, taught her pupils a great deal more. Mornings were spent at geography, history, grammar, and composition. Afternoons were given over to dancing, singing, drawing, and French. Lessons continued even during summer visits to their mother's old home at historic Glamis Castle in Scotland.

When her grandfather died in 1936, Elizabeth watched the funeral procession in solemn silence. Her adored Uncle David was now king and she was second in line for the throne. But the only real change in her small world was that her grandmother now had more time to take her on outings.

Elizabeth was once introduced to an American friend of her uncle's—a certain Mrs. Simpson—but the romance that shook the world was carefully kept from her. When

Edward VIII signed the abdication which made her heiress presumptive, Elizabeth was busy as usual in the schoolroom. The bewildered reaction of the children to their sudden change in rank was voiced by the baby. "I was Margaret of York," she complained, "now I'm just Margaret nothing!"

Elizabeth was soon made aware of her responsibilities. Her father began to spend some time each day training her for the task she would one day assume. The royal dispatch boxes with their important state papers became all too familiar. Otherwise, while all Europe rushed headlong toward the coming disaster, the future queen remained in her schoolroom. Only occasionally did she take part in a state function. But she could not long remain so isolated.

In 1939, Elizabeth and Margaret went to the Royal Naval Academy to meet their parents as they returned from a visit to the United States. One of the cadets assigned as their escort was eighteen-year-old Prince Philip of Greece. Elizabeth was too shy to speak more than a few words to the handsome boy. But from that day forward they wrote to each other.

The war brought many changes. The princesses were evacuated to Balmoral for a while. But they were soon back at Windsor Castle taking refuge in air-raid shelters when the alarms sounded. The lessons in statecraft were resumed. Elizabeth kept busy with her studies, with war sewing and with theatricals to entertain evacuated children. But she felt the need to do more. She begged to be allowed to join some branch of the service like other girls, but to no avail. The nation required of her a service of a very special kind. She assumed the duties of a councillor of state when her father was absent at the front.

It was 1945 before she was finally allowed to join the Auxiliary Territorial Service. As part of her training she learned to drive and service large trucks. Her mother complained that Elizabeth's dinner-table conversation was confined to "sparking plugs," but she did very well.

Then suddenly the war was over. England began to rise from her own ashes. State duties began to take more and more of Elizabeth's time. She drove through miles of bombed-out streets giving aid and comfort to the bereaved and homeless wherever she could. And she made a three-day visit to Ireland, without any member of the family, but with the retinue, of course, that accompanies the state visit of even a young princess.

Now the romance that had been kept alive by infrequent visits and frequent letters blossomed. Philip was seen more and more often at the palace but engagement rumors were denied. Elizabeth was preparing to accompany her parents on a South African tour. In fact, her twenty-first birthday was celebrated there. "Six thousand miles," as she put it, "from the place where I was born, but—certainly not six thousand miles from home."

They returned in May and two months later the engagement was formally announced. On November 20, "A young English girl was married in the family church. You forget the trappings, the plumed helmets, the jeweled orders."

After a honeymoon in Scotland, Elizabeth and Philip, like any newlyweds, began their search for a place to live.

The problem was a little more complicated for them. Finally, it was decided to remodel Clarence House. The princess supervised every detail of the work. She even mixed paints herself in order to get just the right color. She was not, however, allowed to settle down to a life of domestic bliss.

Duty called. In May the bride and groom paid a state visit to France. Both fell ill but, characteristically, never missed an appointment. Then came the announcement that set all tongues to wagging. The Princess Elizabeth would accept no more public engagements. A baby was on the way!

Prince Charles was born November 14, 1947. Almost immediately Elizabeth was back in the public eye. She acted as deputy for her ailing father at such time-honored ceremonies as the trooping of the color. She was able to join Philip for a short time at Gibraltar. He was still a Navy man, and she enjoyed for a few weeks the role of just another Navy wife. He was home, however, when their second child arrived. Like any proud father, he informed the world, "It's the sweetest girl!"

By late summer of 1951 it became clear that only a serious operation offered hope for King George. Elizabeth left on a Canadian tour soon afterward and she carried a sealed envelope which she knew concerned her own accession to the throne. But she did not have to open it. The king's condition improved, and the tour was a rousing success.

The king seemed better. But both Philip and Elizabeth were made members of the Privy Council on their return. Furthermore, they had to set out again almost immediately. They would fill in for the king and queen on a long-promised visit to New Zealand and Australia. But they decided to take a short holiday in Kenya first. One particularly fascinating visit was the Treetops Resthouse. There, Elizabeth spent a happy night watching the wild beasts of Africa in their natural habitat.

It was half past one the next day when Philip gently broke the sad news. King George was dead, and Elizabeth was now Queen of England. In the late afternoon of February 7, 1952, she walked alone down the ramp from her plane to meet her destiny.

No sooner was she proclaimed queen than she plunged into a brutal schedule. In five months she made an astonishing 140 formal appearances. First, of course, came the sad duties connected with her beloved father's funeral. Then came the move to Buckingham Palace. Elizabeth could not bring herself to use her father's familiar study. Another room had to be found for her.

England had come far along the road to recovery, but there was still much to be done. Her shattered economy must be painfully rebuilt. Taxes skyrocketed as the government took on more and more responsibility for the welfare of the people. Social unrest seethed in almost every corner of the far-flung realm.

Elizabeth and England were fortunate in having the services of the man who had led them through their "finest hour," Sir Winston Churchill. He was again Prime Minister during the first crucial years of the new reign. Elizabeth seems to have been truly appreciative of the services of the great statesman who had known her all her life. It was she who insisted on his acceptance of knighthood in the Order of the Garter. And twice she was to break long-standing precedents to do him honor.

The first occasion was in April, 1955. Elizabeth and Philip attended a brilliant dinner at Number 10 Downing Street on the eve of Sir Winston's resignation as Prime Minister. The second came during the mournful days following his death. Elizabeth became the first reigning British monarch to attend the funeral of a commoner. Her floral tribute bore a card inscribed in her own hand: "From the Nation and the Commonwealth in grateful remembrance, Elizabeth, R."

Perhaps she was remembering the loyal old man's remark at her accession. "Famous have been the reigns of our queens."

But these events lay in the future. Meanwhile, Elizabeth's coronation presented many problems. Whether to have TV or not was one of them. It was banned at first and permitted only when the queen expressly desired it. Another was a shortage of royal coaches. It was solved only by borrowing them—and the men to drive them—from the film companies to which they had been sold. Elizabeth's grandmother, Queen Mary, proved an invaluable adviser for the great event. Her death in March, 1953, served to dampen the festive mood.

By June all was in readiness. On the second of that month an entire nation witnessed the solemn and beautiful rites in which a lovely young woman dedicated herself to the service of her country. Almost before the last oath had been sworn and the last peeress had left her place in historic old Westminster Abbey, films had been rushed across the seas so that the whole world might see Elizabeth II become an anointed queen. It was a spectacle few are likely to forget.

Elizabeth left England soon afterward on a fifty-thousand-mile tour. It would carry her through fourteen countries in six months. Everywhere great crowds waited for hours to get a glimpse of her. "Yes! I have seen her," reported one delighted subject. "It has been easy for everyone to see her, and she has been safe, loved, and cherished."

The queen's accessibility doomed her to a grueling pace. On one two-day program she had to be on her feet, smiling graciously, for twenty hours. And she may have set some kind of record by delivering 102 speeches and listening to 200 more in the course of 58 days. She is the first queen to circumnavigate the globe.

A particularly thorny problem greeted her on her return. Princess Margaret had fallen in love with the dashing, much-decorated Group Captain Peter Townsend. He was absolutely unacceptable to the crown because he had been divorced. As head of the Anglican Church, Elizabeth had no choice but to oppose the match, no matter how much she might sympathize with her sister's feelings. Fortunately, Margaret eased the tension by renouncing him. When later she chose young Anthony Armstrong-Jones, the queen did not oppose her sister.

Over the years, Elizabeth has given of herself without stint. She has traveled hundreds of thousands of miles to see and be seen by her subjects. She has entertained almost every person of note in the entire world from heads of state to the Beatles. In all this she has been ably seconded and supported by Philip.

Seldom have they had any time to themselves. Occasionally, they can combine pleasure with business and take a holiday tour after a formal visit abroad. Thus, a state visit to Sweden was timed to coincide with the equestrian events of the 1956 Olympics. Elizabeth had the thrill of seeing one of her own horses make a gallant run. And she cheered the English team as it took the gold medal.

The queen's interest in racing is one of her few relaxations. She is an ardent horsewoman and an excellent one. She kept a "stable" of wooden horses as a child. And she once told Crawfie that if she didn't have to be a princess she rather thought she would like to be a horse.

Like her sister queen, Juliana, Elizabeth has seen many changes and met many crises during her reign. The empire of Victoria has dwindled. Independence granted to colony after colony has left the empire a mere shadow of its former self. Many, however, remain in the British Commonwealth of Nations and do homage to Elizabeth as their sovereign.

Over the years, two more princes have made their appearance. Elizabeth and Philip have given much thought to the education of their children. Prince Charles, who will one day inherit his mother's throne, has been given as normal an upbringing as possible. Far from being coddled, he was sent to one of the most rigorous schools in England. Though rather shy, he seems a well-adjusted young man. Britons seem to think he will do very well.

Meanwhile his parents continue their marathon of tours and public functions. One brief visit to the United States included a football game, a speech at the UN, a visit to a supermarket, a dinner for four thousand guests, a trip to the Empire State Building, a ticker-tape parade, and a

Commonwealth Ball. "Strong men have broken, covering this royal runaway," wrote reporter Bob Considine. "There isn't a clear eye left, except Elizabeth's." Elizabeth, in fact, had a lovely time.

Elizabeth—and the whole concept of monarchy—have many critics among the English. But few who come in contact with this gracious and truly regal woman can fail to respect her. She has a genuine and intelligent interest in the welfare of her realm and a knack for making each person feel as though he alone mattered.

Most Englishmen are uttering a sincere wish as they raise their voices to sing "God Save the Queen."

# Bibliography

Anthony, Katherine S., *Catherine the Great*, New York, Alfred A. Knopf, 1925.

Bolitho, Hector, *The Reign of Queen Victoria*, New York, The Macmillan Company, 1948.

Breasted, James Henry, *A History of Egypt*, New York, Bantam Books, 1964 (published originally by Scribner's, 1905).

Chanler, Beatrice, *Cleopatra's Daughter*, New York, Liveright, 1934.

Costain, Thomas B., *The Conquering Family*, New York, Popular Library, 1964.

Dark, Sidney, *Twelve Royal Ladies*, New York, Thomas Y. Crowell, 1929.

# Bibliography

Diehl, Charles, *Byzantine Empresses*, New York, Alfred A. Knopf, 1963.

Farmer, Lydia, *A Book of Famous Queens*, New York, Thomas Y. Crowell, 1964 (revised).

Gibbon, Edward, *Decline and Fall of the Roman Empire*, Great Books Edition, Chicago, *Encyclopædia Britannica*, 1952.

Goodrich, Frank B., *World Famous Women*, Philadelphia, Ziegler, 1881.

Grey, Ian, *Catherine the Great; Autocrat and Empress of All the Russias*, Philadelphia, Lippincott, 1962.

Henderson, Daniel, *The Crimson Queen*, New York, Duffield & Green, 1933.

Heritier, Jean, *Catherine de' Medici*, New York, Saint Martin's Press, 1959.

Hornblow, Leonora, *Cleopatra of Egypt*, New York, Random House, 1961.

Hussey, Harry, *Venerable Ancestor*, Garden City, N. Y., Doubleday, 1949.

Jenkins, Elizabeth M., *Elizabeth the Great*, New York, Coward McCann, 1959.

Kelley, Amy Ruth, *Eleanor of Aquitaine and the Four Kings*, Cambridge, Mass., Harvard University Press, 1950.

Larsen, *History of Norway*, Princeton, N. J., Princeton University Press, 1948.

Lewis, Paul, *Queen of Caprice*, London, Alvin Redman, 1962.

Longford, Elizabeth, *Queen Victoria; Born to Succeed*, New York, Harper & Row, 1964.

Ludwig, Emil, *Cleopatra*, New York, Viking Press, 1937.

McKenzie, F. C., *Sybil of the North*, New York, Houghton Mifflin, 1931.

Morris, Constance L., *Maria Theresa; the Last Conservative*, New York, Alfred A. Knopf, 1937.

Morrison, N. Brysson, *Mary, Queen of Scots,* New York, Vanguard Press, 1960.

*The National Geographic* "Everyday Life in Ancient Times," Washington, D.C., The National Geographic Society, 1951.

Oldenbourg, Zoe, *Catharine the Great,* New York, Random House, 1965.

Pearson, Hesketh, *Henry of Navarre,* New York, Harper & Row, 1963.

Prescott, William H., *History of the Reign of Ferdinand and Isabella the Catholic,* Philadelphia, Lippincott, 1873.

Roeder, Ralph, *Catherine de' Medici and the Lost Revolution,* New York, Viking Press, 1937.

Rosenberg, *Eleanor of Aquitaine; Queen of the Troubadours and the Courts of Love,* Boston, Houghton Mifflin, 1937.

Saunders, Beatrice, *Henry the Eighth,* London, Alvin Redman, 1963.

Tacitus, *The Annals,* Great Books Edition, Chicago, *Encyclopædia Britannica,* 1952.

Tisdall, Evelyn, *Queen Victoria's Private Life,* New York, John Day, 1961.

Van Dyke, Paul, *Catherine de Medicis,* New York, Charles Scribner's Sons, 1922.

Volkmann, Hans, *Cleopatra,* New York, Sagamore Press, 1958.

Walker, Curtis H., *Eleanor of Aquitaine,* University of North Carolina Press, 1950.

Warner, W. L., *King John,* New Yok, W. W. Norton, 1961.

Wilhelmina, Queen of the Netherlands, *Lonely but Not Alone,* New York, McGraw-Hill, 1960.

Withers, E. L., *Royal Blood,* Garden City, N. Y., Doubelday, 1964.

# INDEX

# Rulers In Petticoats

# Index

( 223 )